Storms and Hurricanes

Emily Bone

Illustrated by Paul Weston

Designed by Alice Reese and Sam Chandler

Additional illustrations by Kimberley Scott
Storms consultant: Dr. Roger Trend
Reading consultant: Alison Kelly, Principal Lecturer at the University of Roehampton

Contents

- 3 Stormy skies
- 4 Different weather
- 6 Cloudy skies
- 8 Wild winds
- 10 Cold storms
- 12 Ice storms
- 14 Electric skies
- 16 Whirling winds
- 18 Dry storms
- 20 The biggest storm
- 22 During the storm
- 24 After the storm
- 26 Tracking storms
- 28 Strange storms
- 30 Glossary
- 31 Websites to visit
- 32 Index

Stormy skies

During a storm, there are thick, dark clouds in the sky, very strong winds and often heavy rain or snow.

Sometimes, there is thunder and lightning, too.

This is a big storm in Nebraska, U.S.A.

Different weather

Storms and other kinds of weather happen all over the world. Weather is formed in the air that surrounds the Earth.

You can see weather from space. This picture shows white, swirling clouds.

The gaps between the clouds are clear skies.

The type of weather depends on how hot, cold, dry or damp the air is.

Where the air is hot and dry, the weather is sunny and there's no rain.

Cold and damp air makes cloudy, foggy, rainy or snowy weather.

Many storms happen where the air becomes hot and damp.

Other planets such as Jupiter have storms, too.

Cloudy skies

Storm clouds form when the air is warm and damp. Damp air is filled with very tiny water droplets, so small you can't see them.

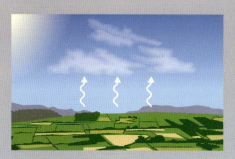

1. The Sun shines and heats up the air making the water droplets rise.

2. High above the ground, the droplets cool and join together to make clouds.

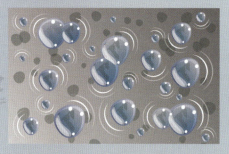

3. Inside the cloud, the droplets bump together and join to form bigger droplets.

4. Soon, the droplets of water are so big and heavy that they fall as rain.

In some parts of the world, so much rain falls at once, the ground floods.

This is Calcutta in India. It rains like this for around two months every year.

In some parts of Hawaii, U.S.A., it rains almost every day.

Wild winds

All storms come with strong winds. Wind is moving air. It happens when hot air rises and cold air rushes in to take its place.

Very strong storm winds are called gales.

These waves are crashing onto the land during a gale. Land close to the sea is often flooded.

Gales are so strong that it can be difficult for people to stand up.

Tiles are blown from roofs, and trees and electricity pylons are knocked over.

Huge waves form at sea making it very dangerous for ships and their crews.

Palm trees can bend in strong winds so they don't get blown over.

Cold storms

Snowstorms happen when the air is very cold.

Water droplets in clouds freeze into tiny ice crystals, called snowflakes.

More droplets freeze onto the flakes until they're too heavy to stay up.

Lots of snowflakes fall, covering the ground in a thick layer of snow.

This is a snowstorm in Washington D.C., U.S.A. Snow has filled the sky, making it difficult to see anything.

A snowstorm with very strong winds is called a blizzard.

Ice storms

Small balls of ice, called hailstones, form when water droplets are blown around inside a storm cloud.

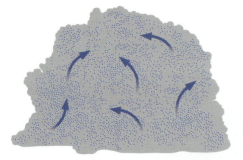

1. Droplets are blown around the cloud, where they freeze into hailstones.

2. The hailstones are blown around more. They get covered in a layer of water.

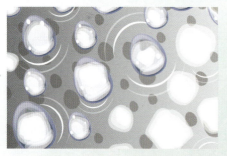

3. The water freezes into a layer around the hailstones, and they get bigger.

4. Eventually, the hailstones are so heavy, they fall to the ground.

When lots of hailstones fall from a storm cloud, it's called a hailstorm.

This giant hailstone fell in Kansas, U.S.A. It is shown here at around half its actual size.

If you cut a hailstone open, you would see the different frozen layers.

Electric skies

Thunder and lightning form inside massive storm clouds.

Damp, warm air rises high into the sky. As it cools, it turns into a storm cloud.

Inside the cloud, the wind swirls a mixture of hailstones and rain up and down.

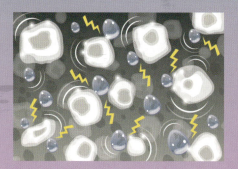

The hailstones and rain bump and rub against each other. This makes electricity.

The electricity leaps down from the cloud as a very hot flash of lightning.

Thunder is the sound of the air quickly heating up around the lightning flash.

When lightning splits like this, it is called forked lightning.

Light travels faster than sound, so you always see lightning before you hear thunder.

Whirling winds

Tornadoes are extremely fast, spinning winds that form inside storm clouds. In some places, they are called twisters.

A tornado's violent winds can destroy houses and farmland. This is a tornado in the U.S.A.

1. The air inside a storm cloud slowly starts to spin around and around.

2. The air spins faster and faster. The bottom of the cloud starts to grow.

3. Air is sucked up from the ground. It turns into a whirling funnel of cloud.

4. As the tornado moves along the ground it causes serious damage.

Tornadoes are called twisters because they can twist the tops from trees.

Dry storms

Dust storms happen in very hot, windy places where there is no rain, such as deserts.

The Sun bakes the ground, making it very dry. The soil cracks into pieces.

Loose pieces of soil are blown along the ground, making them break up even more.

Soon, the loose soil becomes fine dust and strong winds blow it into huge clouds.

Camels can close their noses so that they don't breathe in dust during a dust storm.

This is a dust storm in Afghanistan. The dust has filled the sky, blocking out the Sun.

The biggest storm

Hurricanes are huge, violent storms with very strong winds and heavy rain. They form over warm seas and can blow onto land.

The Sun heats moist air over the sea.

The moist air rises very quickly. Then it starts to spin.

As it spins, the air creates big, swirling storm clouds.

The storm gets bigger and bigger and grows into a hurricane.

This is what a hurricane looks like from space. The middle of the storm is called the eye.

In different countries, hurricanes are also known as cyclones, typhoons and willy-willies.

During the storm

Different parts of a hurricane produce different types of weather.

These palm trees in Florida, U.S.A., are being whipped by winds from a hurricane.

1. At the start of a hurricane, big swirls of dark clouds form in the sky.

2. Extremely strong winds blow, and there is heavy rain, hail, and thunder and lightning.

3. As the eye of the storm passes overhead, it is clear and sunny.

4. When the eye has moved on, clouds fill the sky. The violent weather starts again.

After the storm

When a hurricane strikes an area, it causes serious damage.

This is New Orleans, U.S.A., after Hurricane Katrina in 2005. Strong winds destroyed thousands of houses.

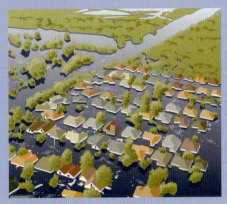

Hurricane winds create big waves that damage buildings on the shore.

Heavy rain makes rivers overflow their banks, flooding large areas of land.

Tracking storms

Scientists study storms to find out more about why they happen.

This weather truck has stopped under a storm cloud in Oklahoma, U.S.A.

The truck has equipment to measure wind, rain and temperature in the clouds.

Weather satellites in space look for hurricanes forming at sea.

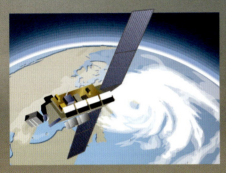

Satellites send information about the hurricane to a control room.

Computers find out where and when the hurricane might reach land.

Flags are put up in danger areas. There are warnings on the radio and television.

People leave their homes quickly so they can escape the hurricane.

Strange storms

In some parts of the world, stormy weather can do unusual things.

During an ice storm, heavy rain falls onto very cold surfaces and freezes. This photo was taken after an ice storm in Switzerland.

A tornado's strong winds can pick up fish, frogs and other small animals.

The animals are carried along, then dropped, as if they're raining from the sky.

Glossary

Here are some of the words in this book you might not know. This page tells you what they mean.

 lightning - a hot flash of electricity that jumps down from a storm cloud.

 thunder - the loud rumbling sound following a lightning flash.

 hail - small balls of ice that form inside a storm cloud.

 tornado - very fast spinning winds that look like a funnel of cloud.

 dust storm - when dry soil is blown into big clouds, blocking out the Sun.

 hurricane - a massive, violent storm with very strong winds and heavy rain.

 weather satellite - a machine in space that detects hurricanes forming.

Websites to visit

You can visit exciting websites to find out more about storms.

To visit these websites, go to the Usborne Quicklinks Website at **www.usborne-quicklinks.com** Read the internet safety guidelines, and then type the keywords "**beginners storms**".

The websites are regularly reviewed and the links in Usborne Quicklinks are updated. However, Usborne Publishing is not responsible, and does not accept liability, for the content or availability of any website other than its own. We recommend that children are supervised while on the internet.

This is a whirling cloud of dust, called a dust devil. It's made by extremely fast, spinning winds close to the ground, like a small tornado.

Index

blizzards, 11
clouds, 3, 4, 5, 6, 10, 12, 14, 16, 17, 19, 20, 22, 23, 26
dust storms, 18-19, 30
electricity, 14
flooding, 7, 8, 25
gales, 8, 9
hail, 12-13, 14, 22, 30
hurricanes, 20-25, 27, 30
ice storms, 28
lightning, 3, 14-15, 30
rain, 3, 5, 6-7, 14, 22, 25, 26
sea, 8, 9, 20, 25, 27
snow, 3, 10-11
storm damage, 7, 8, 9, 16, 17, 24-25
Sun, 5, 6, 18, 19, 20
thunder, 3, 14, 15, 30
tornadoes, 16-17, 29, 30
warning, 27
water droplets, 6, 10, 12
weather satellites, 27, 30
wind, 3, 8, 9, 11, 12, 14, 16-17, 18, 19, 20, 22, 24, 25, 26, 29, 31

Acknowledgements

Photographic manipulation by Mike Olley
Additional design by Will Dawes

Photo credits

The publishers are grateful to the following for permission to reproduce material: cover © Gene Rhoden/Weatherpix/Getty Images; p1© Lyle Leduc/Getty Images; p2-3 © Mike Hollingshead/Getty Images; p4 © NASA/NOAA/GSFC/Suomi NPP/VIIRS/Norman Kuring; p7 © Frederic Soltan/Sygma/Corbis; p8 © Natureslight/Alamy; p11 © ABACA USA/Press Association images; p13 © nagelestock.com/Alamy; p15 © NCAR/Science Photo Library; p16 © imagedepotpro/Getty Images; p18-19 © Ahmad Masood/Reuters/Corbis; p21 © Fotosearch/SuperStock; p22-23 © Burton McNeely/Getty Images; p24-25 © age fotostock/SuperStock; p26 © Josh Wurman; p28-29 © Prisma Bildagentur AG/Alamy; p31 © John Warburton-Lee Photography/Alamy.

Every effort has been made to trace and acknowledge ownership of copyright. If any rights have been omitted, the publishers offer to rectify this in any subsequent editions following notification.

First published in 2012 by Usborne Publishing Ltd., Usborne House, 83-85 Saffron Hill, London EC1N 8RT, England. www.usborne.com Copyright © 2012 Usborne Publishing Ltd. The name Usborne and the devices ♀⊕ are Trade Marks of Usborne Publishing Ltd. All rights reserved. No part of this publication may be reproduced, stored in a retrieval system, or transmitted in any form or by any means, electronic, mechanical, photocopying, recording or otherwise without the prior permission of the publisher.
First published in America 2012. U.E.

Earthquakes
and Tsunamis

Emily Bone

Illustrated by Natalie Hinrichsen

Designed by Will Dawes, Lucy Wain and Zöe Wray

Additional illustrations by Nicola Slater

Earthquake consultant: Dr. Roger Trend

Reading consultant: Alison Kelly, Principal Lecturer at the University of Roehampton

Contents

- 3   Shaking earth
- 4   Moving rock
- 6   Faults
- 8   How does it feel?
- 10 Slipping land
- 12 City destruction
- 14 After the quake
- 16 Helping people
- 18 Earthquakes at sea
- 20 Tsunami warning
- 22 San Francisco shock
- 24 Staying safe
- 26 Earthquake drills
- 28 When will it happen?
- 30 Glossary
- 31 Websites to visit
- 32 Index

Shaking earth

During an earthquake, the ground suddenly trembles. Earthquakes can happen on land or under the sea.

Some earthquakes shake the ground violently. An earthquake has made the big cracks in these roads in Haiti.

Moving rock

The Earth is made of rock. Inside the Earth, there is very hot rock that moves around very, very slowly.

The Earth's surface is made up of big pieces of hard rock, called plates.

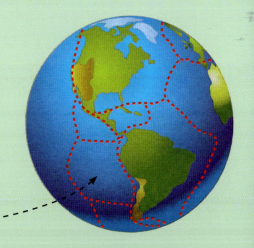

A plate

The plates move around on top of the hot rock.

As they move, some plates push against each other. Others pull apart.

When plates push against each other for millions of years, they form mountains.

Here are the edges of two plates in Iceland. The plates are moving away from each other, in opposite directions.

The gap made in the Earth's surface is called a rift.

Faults

Most earthquakes happen where two plates scrape against each other.

In some places there are cracks near the edges of the plates, called faults.

This is the San Andreas fault in California, U.S.A. Over 10,000 earthquakes happen along its length, every year.

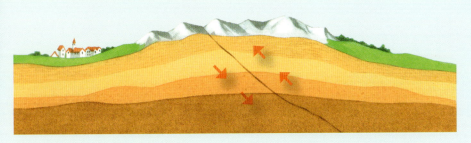

Sections of rock in a fault shift and push against each other.

Sometimes, a big section of rock suddenly slips, making the surrounding rock shake.

The shaking spreads up to the surface, causing an earthquake.

As the rock in a fault settles after a big earthquake it can cause smaller quakes, called aftershocks.

How does it feel?

When an earthquake starts, the ground trembles, then shakes violently. The effects of an earthquake are measured on a scale. The most famous is called the Richter scale.

0 means that the ground is completely still.

At levels 4 to 5, windows rattle. Things are thrown off shelves and walls.

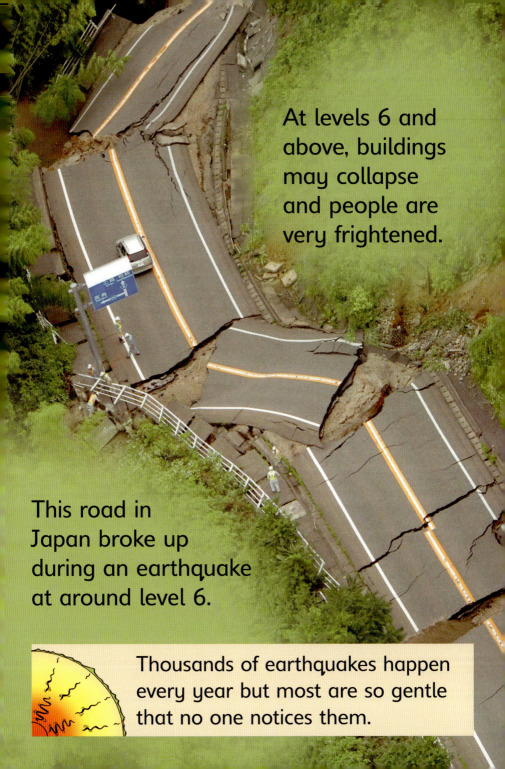

At levels 6 and above, buildings may collapse and people are very frightened.

This road in Japan broke up during an earthquake at around level 6.

Thousands of earthquakes happen every year but most are so gentle that no one notices them.

Slipping land

Earthquakes also loosen big sections of soil and rock, making them slip down steep slopes. This is called a landslide.

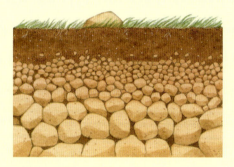

Usually, soil and rocks on the ground are packed closely together.

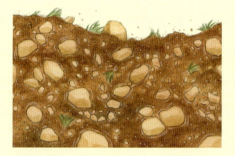

When the ground shakes, the rocks and soil are shaken apart.

On a slope, the loose rocks slide down very quickly, pushing more rocks and soil down, too.

Part of this hill in China has fallen away during a landslide. The rocks have smashed into houses at the bottom.

City destruction

When a big earthquake strikes in a city, it causes serious damage, and puts peoples' lives in danger.

Buildings are shaken in all directions, making their walls crack and collapse.

Electricity cables fall down, so people don't have any power, light or heat.

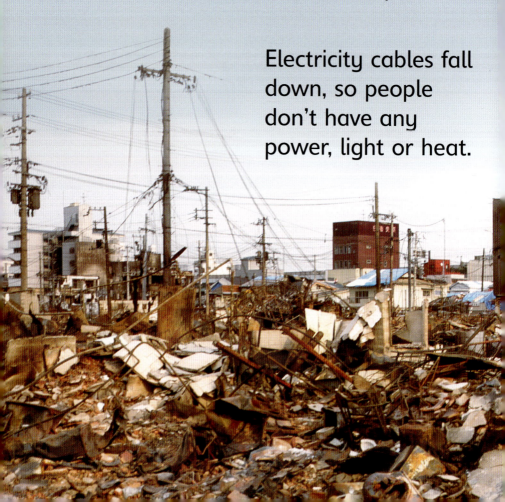

The trembling ground makes roads and bridges break up.

Water pipes burst open, cutting off water supplies to the city.

This is a city in Japan after a violent earthquake.

After the quake

Rescue teams find people who are trapped and in danger after an earthquake.

This rescuer is using a dog to find people under buildings that collapsed during an earthquake in Japan.

The dog can find people by smelling them.

Rescuers use equipment to free people quickly and safely.

A rescuer pushes a small camera on a long pole through the rubble.

The camera is linked to a screen that shows if a person is trapped.

Rescuers carefully take away pieces of rubble to make a hole.

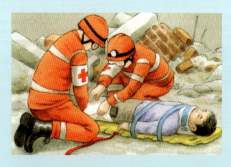

The person is lifted out of the hole and strapped onto a stretcher.

Helping people

When earthquakes damage houses and shops, people can be left with nowhere to live and no way to look after themselves.

To help people, emergency camps are set up, like this one in Pakistan. There are tents for people to sleep in.

People staying in the camp are given food, water, blankets and clothes.

Camp schools are set up so children don't miss their lessons.

Earthquakes at sea

When earthquakes happen under the sea they can create gigantic waves, called tsunamis. This is how they are made.

1. An earthquake jolts the sea floor up and down.

2. The sea above it is jolted, too. Waves form on the surface.

3. Waves start to race towards the shore, gradually getting bigger and more powerful.

Tsunamis are so powerful, they can carry huge ships far inland.

4. Massive waves crash onto the shore with enough force to destroy buildings and trees.

Tsunami warning

A tsunami can flood large areas of land.

Here, a tsunami in Indonesia has destroyed a village that is a long way from the sea.

In tsunami danger areas, there are warning systems to help people get to safety quickly.

Machines detect an earthquake at sea and send signals to a control room.

Computers in the control room find out where a tsunami may happen.

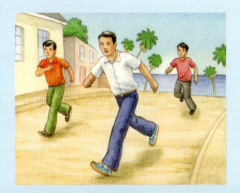

Alarms sound in the places in danger. People run to high ground.

San Francisco shock

San Francisco in California, U.S.A, is close to the San Andreas fault. On April 18, 1906, a major earthquake struck the city.

The shaking was so violent, many buildings collapsed. This photograph shows San Francisco a week after the earthquake.

Power lines broke, causing huge fires that destroyed most of the city.

People who had lost their homes were moved to big, temporary camps.

Staying safe

In some areas where earthquakes happen, there are new ways to protect people during an earthquake.

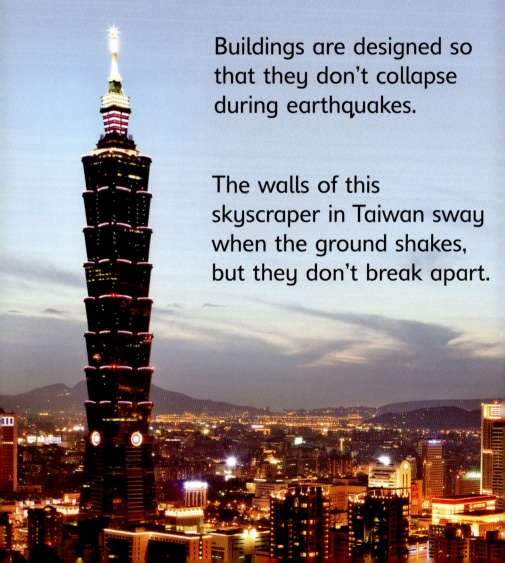

Buildings are designed so that they don't collapse during earthquakes.

The walls of this skyscraper in Taiwan sway when the ground shakes, but they don't break apart.

Some houses are built on stilts to stop them from being flooded by tsunamis.

Here are some ways that people prepare so they can stay safe during an earthquake.

Heavy furniture is attached to walls so it doesn't fall over and hurt people.

Families arrange a safe place to meet in case they get split up.

People keep a kit of emergency supplies such as fresh water and blankets.

Earthquake drills

People living in danger of earthquakes rehearse what to do if an earthquake starts when they're at school or work.

These school children in Japan are learning how to shelter under their desks. This would stop them from being hurt by falling objects.

For the next part of the drill, the children calmly walk out of the building in a line.

They wear padded hoods as this would protect their heads during an earthquake.

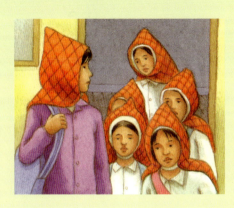

Everyone gathers in an open space, away from trees and buildings.

They crouch down so they wouldn't be knocked over if the ground shook.

When will it happen?

No one knows for certain when or where an earthquake will happen.

Scientists study faults as they think movements in the rock may help them to predict earthquakes.

Here, scientists are using powerful beams of light to detect any movement.

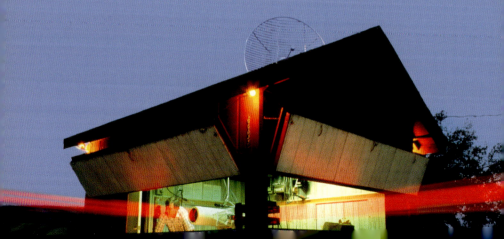

Some people believe that there are other ways to predict an earthquake.

Sometimes, dogs bark and run outside just before an earthquake starts.

Frogs and other animals may leave an area days before an earthquake hits.

Flashes of light in the sky could mean an earthquake is about to happen.

Glossary

Here are some of the words in this book you might not know. This page tells you what they mean.

 plate - a big piece of moving rock. Plates make up the Earth's surface.

 faults - cracks in the rock along plate edges where earthquakes happen.

 landslide - when big sections of soil and rocks slip downhill.

 emergency camp - a place people can stay if their homes are destroyed.

 tsunami - massive waves formed when there is an earthquake at sea.

 warning system - a system to detect tsunamis so people can get to safety.

 earthquake drill - a rehearsal of what to do during and after an earthquake.

Websites to visit

You can visit exciting websites to find out more about earthquakes and tsunamis.

To visit these websites, go to the Usborne Quicklinks Website at **www.usborne-quicklinks.com** Read the internet safety guidelines, and then type the keywords "**beginners earthquakes**".

The websites are regularly reviewed and the links in Usborne Quicklinks are updated. However, Usborne Publishing is not responsible, and does not accept liability, for the content or availability of any website other than its own. We recommend that children are supervised while on the internet.

A powerful tsunami in Indonesia washed these houses onto a beach.

Index

animals, 14, 29
buildings, 9, 11, 12, 13, 14, 16, 19, 20, 22, 23, 24, 25, 27, 31
camps, 16-17, 23, 30
cities, 12-13, 22, 23
detection, 21, 28-29
drills, 26-27, 30
Earth, 4, 5
emergency supplies, 17, 25
faults, 6-7, 22, 28, 30
flooding, 20, 25
landslides, 10-11, 30
people, 9, 14, 15, 16, 17, 21, 23, 24, 25, 26, 27
plates, 4-5, 6, 30
power, 12, 23
rescue teams, 14-15
roads, 3, 9, 13
rocks, 4, 7, 10, 11, 28
safety, 15, 21, 24-25, 26, 27
schools, 17, 26
sea, 3, 18, 19, 20, 21
shaking, 3, 7, 8, 12, 13, 24, 27
tsunamis, 18-19, 20, 21, 25, 30, 31

Acknowledgements

Photographic manipulation by Nick Wakeford
With thanks to Ruth King and Sam Lake

Photo credits

The publishers are grateful to the following for permission to reproduce material:
cover © **TWPhoto/Corbis**; p1 © **2011 AFP/Getty**; p2-3 © **Robert Harding World Imagery/Alamy**; p5 © **Robert Harding Travel/Photolibrary (Geoff Renner)**;
p6 © **Peter Arnold Images/Photolibrary (Kevin Schafer)**; p 8 © **Kyodo/X01481/Reuters/Corbis**;
p9 © **Niigata-Nippo/Hiroshi Sekine/Reuters/Corbis**; p11 © **Jason Lee/Reuters/Corbis**;
p12-13 © **Michael S. Yamashita/Corbis**; p14 © **Ria Novosti**; p16-17 © **Goran Tomasevic/Reuters/Corbis**; p18-19, p30 (tsunami entry) © **Gary Hinks/Science Photo Library**; p20 © **Stephen J. Boitano/Alamy**; p22-23 © **US National Archive, 111-AGF-1A-1D**; p24 © **Tom Bonaventure/Getty**;
p26 © **AFP/Getty Images**; p29 © **David Parker/Science Photo Library**;
p31 © **Trinity Mirror/Mirrorpix/Alamy**.

Every effort has been made to trace and acknowledge ownership of copyright. If any rights have been omitted, the publishers offer to rectify this in any subsequent editions following notification.

First published in 2012 by Usborne Publishing Ltd., Usborne House, 83-85 Saffron Hill, London EC1N 8RT, England. www.usborne.com Copyright © 2012 Usborne Publishing Ltd. The name Usborne and the devices ♀ ⊕ are Trade Marks of Usborne Publishing Ltd. All rights reserved. No part of this publication may be reproduced, stored in a retrieval system, or transmitted in any form or by any means, electronic, mechanical, photocopying, recording or otherwise without the prior permission of the publisher.
First published in America 2012. U.E.

The Solar System

Emily Bone

Designed by Helen Edmonds and Will Dawes
Illustrated by Terry Pastor and Tim Haggerty

Solar System consultant: Stuart Atkinson
Reading consultant: Alison Kelly, Principal Lecturer at Roehampton University

Contents

- 3   In space
- 4   What's out there?
- 6   How it started
- 8   In the middle
- 10   Moving planets
- 12   Mercury
- 14   Hot planet
- 16   Living Earth
- 18   Bright at night
- 20   The red planet
- 22   Gas giant
- 24   Ringed planet
- 26   Distant planets
- 28   Exploring the sky
- 30   Glossary
- 31   Websites to visit
- 32   Index

In space

The Earth is a planet. It's a huge, round lump of rock floating in space.

The Earth is one of eight planets that travel around the Sun. The Sun and the planets are called the Solar System.

This is what the Earth looks like from space.

What's out there?

The planets in the Solar System move around the Sun.

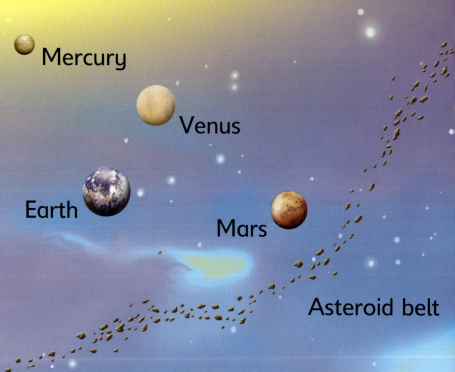

The Sun

Mercury

Venus

Earth

Mars

Asteroid belt

Pieces of rock, called asteroids, travel around the Sun, too.

The planets are shown close together on these pages. Really, they are very, very far apart.

Jupiter

Saturn

Uranus

Neptune

As well as planets, there are lots of other things that move around the Sun, from specks of dust to 'dwarf planets' such as Pluto.

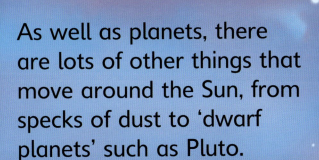

Pluto

How it started

Scientists think that the Solar System formed millions and millions of years ago.

It began as a huge cloud of gas and dust in space, like this one.

The swirling cloud of gas and dust slowly got thicker and thicker.

Part of the cloud heated up, making a hot ball of gas. This became the Sun.

Over millions of years, the gas and dust spun around the Sun.

Gradually, the dust and gas joined together to make the planets.

In the middle

The Sun is a massive ball of burning gas called a star. It gives the planets all their light and heat.

The Sun looks so big because it is closer to the Earth than other stars.

This is what its surface looks like close up.

Jets of hot gas shoot out and fall back in long loops.

Some parts of the Sun are not as hot as the rest. These are called sunspots.

Huge explosions are known as solar flares.

Never look directly at the Sun. Its light is so strong it could damage your eyes.

Moving planets

Each planet travels along its own path, or orbit, around the Sun. They take different lengths of time to move all of the way around.

Earth takes 365 days and nights to orbit the Sun. This is one year.

As the planets travel, they also spin around. When each planet spins, different parts have day or night.

Light from the Sun only shines on one side of the Earth at any time.

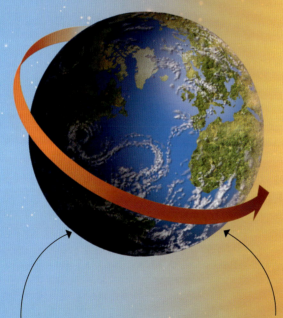

This part is dark because the Sun's light cannot reach it. This is night.

The parts facing the Sun are lit up. This is the planet's day.

Mercury

Mercury is the planet closest to the Sun.

Its rocky surface is covered in holes called craters. Most of these were made by rocks crashing into the planet from space.

Fast-moving rocks hit Mercury's surface making deep holes.

Lots of pieces of rock and dust flew up around the holes.

The rock and dust settled in thick layers around the craters.

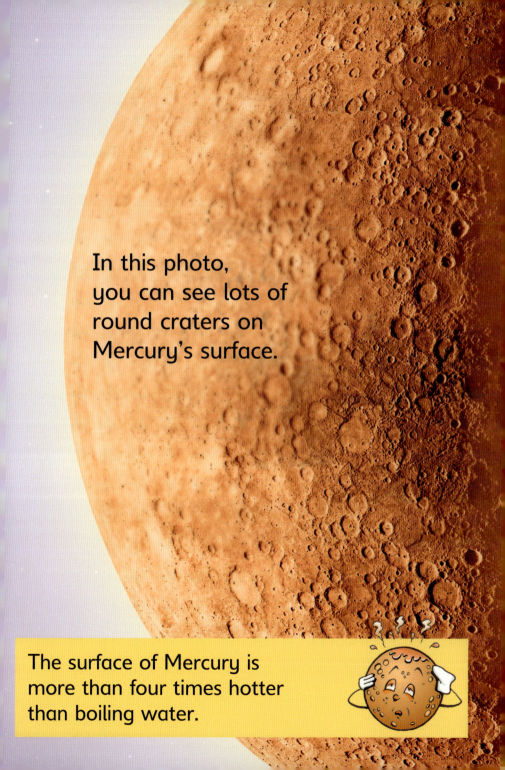

In this photo, you can see lots of round craters on Mercury's surface.

The surface of Mercury is more than four times hotter than boiling water.

Hot planet

Venus is the hottest planet in the Solar System. It is so hot because it is covered in a thick layer of clouds.

This is the surface of Venus. The thick clouds make the sky look orange.

The surface of the planet is hard rock.

 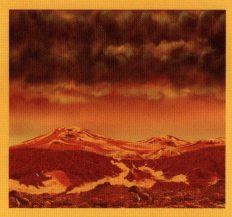

The Sun's rays pass through the clouds and the planet's surface warms up.

The clouds stop the heat from escaping so the planet gets hotter and hotter.

Venus is so hot its surface glows in the dark.

Living Earth

The Earth is made of rock and is surrounded by water and gases. It is the only planet where life is known to exist.

The Earth has the right mixture of air, heat and water for things to live.

A layer of gases around Earth gives living things the air they need to breathe.

In this photo, you can see big lakes and high, rocky mountains on Earth's surface.

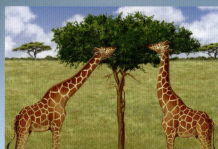

The Sun warms the planet. Plants grow in sunlight, making food for animals.

More than half of the Earth is covered in water. Everything needs water to live.

Bright at night

The Moon is a big, round lump of rock that moves around the Earth. It is the brightest thing you can see in the night sky.

There are millions of craters on the Moon. In this photo, the biggest craters look like dark patches.

As the Moon moves, the Sun lights up different parts of its surface. This is why the Moon seems to change shape.

When the side facing Earth is lit up, you can see the Moon as a bright circle.

Sometimes, you can only see part of the side that is lit by the Sun.

When the Sun shines behind the Moon you can't see the bright side, so it looks dark.

In 1969, astronauts landed on the Moon in a spacecraft.

The red planet

Mars is a cold and rocky planet. Its surface is covered in red dust. Scientists have sent vehicles called rovers to Mars to take photos of the surface.

A rover was packed inside a spacecraft and flown from Earth to Mars.

Air bags protected the spacecraft as it landed on the planet's surface.

This is a photo of Mars' surface, taken by a rover.

Dust storms on Mars can last for months.

The spacecraft opened up and scientists sent signals to drive the rover out.

The rover drove around, sending information back to scientists on Earth.

Gas giant

Jupiter is the biggest planet in the Solar System. It is a huge, round mass made mostly from gases.

The stripes you can see here are bands of different gases.

Jupiter has over 60 moons moving around it. All the moons are made of rock and ice.

 Thebe is not round like most moons. Its surface is covered in huge craters.

The rocky surface of Europa is completely covered in a layer of ice.

Ganymede is the biggest moon in the Solar System. It is bigger than Mercury.

There is a huge storm on Jupiter that has been raging for thousands of years.

Ringed planet

Saturn is a huge planet made mostly of gases. It has millions of pieces of rock and ice moving around it. From far away, these look like solid rings.

This photo was taken from a spacecraft that scientists sent to fly around Saturn.

In 1997, a rocket took off from Earth. It was controlled by computers.

When the rocket was far above the Earth, a probe flew away from it.

The probe reached Saturn and started to fly around and around the planet.

It sent close-up pictures of Saturn and its rings back to Earth.

Distant planets

Uranus and Neptune are huge gas planets.

This is Uranus. It has faint rings around it made from millions of specks of dust.

Uranus spins differently from the other planets. It looks as if it has been knocked on its side.

Neptune is a very cold and stormy planet. This dark blue swirl is a storm raging on the planet.

Beyond Neptune, there is a dwarf planet called Pluto. Experts used to think it was a planet but they've changed their minds.

Exploring the sky

Scientists find out about the Solar System by using huge telescopes that let them see things that are very far away.

The telescopes shown here are in Hawaii, U.S.A. They use big, curved mirrors to make things that are far away look a lot bigger.

There are some telescopes that travel around the Earth in space.

1. Scientists on Earth send signals to point the telescope at a planet.

2. The telescope takes pictures of the planet and stores them in a computer.

3. The computer sends the pictures as signals to huge radio dishes on Earth.

4. The information is sent to computers that turn them into pictures of the planet.

Glossary

Here are some of the words in this book you might not know. This page tells you what they mean.

 planet - a huge mass of rock or gas in space that moves around the Sun.

 asteroid - a lump of rock that moves around the Sun.

 orbit - the path of something as it goes around something else.

 crater - a round hole on a planet or moon made by a rock crashing into it.

 rover - a computer-controlled vehicle that drives across a planet.

 probe - a computer-controlled spacecraft sent to explore space.

 telescope - something that makes things that are far away look bigger.

Websites to visit

You can visit exciting websites to find out more about the Solar System.

To visit these websites, go to the Usborne Quicklinks Website at **www.usborne-quicklinks.com** Read the internet safety guidelines, and then type the keywords "**beginners solar system**".

The websites are regularly reviewed and the links in Usborne Quicklinks are updated. However, Usborne Publishing is not responsible, and does not accept liability, for the content or availability of any website other than its own. We recommend that children are supervised while on the internet.

This is the International Space Station. Scientists live on it and do experiments to find out more about space.

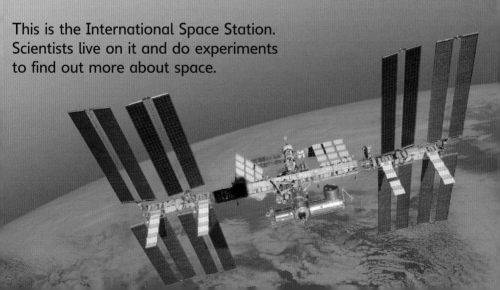

Index

asteroids, 4, 30
craters, 12, 13, 18, 23, 30
dust, 5, 6, 7, 12, 20, 21, 26
dwarf planets, 5, 27
Earth, 3, 4, 8, 10, 11, 16-17, 18, 20, 21, 24, 25, 29
gas, 6, 7, 8, 16, 22, 24
ice, 23, 24
Jupiter, 5, 22-23,
Mars, 4, 20-21
Mercury, 4, 12-13, 23
moons, 18, 19, 23
Neptune, 5, 26, 27
orbits, 10, 30
Pluto, 5, 27
probes, 24, 25, 30
rings, 24-25, 26
rock, 3, 12, 14, 16, 17, 18, 20, 23, 24
rovers, 20-21, 30
Saturn, 5, 24-25
scientists, 6, 20, 21, 24, 28, 29, 31
spacecraft, 19, 20, 21, 24, 25, 31
Sun, 3, 4, 5, 6, 7, 8-9, 10, 11, 12, 15, 17, 19
telescopes, 28-29, 30
Uranus, 5, 26
Venus, 4, 14-15
water, 13, 16, 17, 23

Acknowledgements

Photographic manipulation by John Russell

Photo credits

The publishers are grateful to the following for permission to reproduce material:
© Chris Knorr/Design Pics Inc./Corbis **28**; © Design Pics Inc./Photolibrary **18** (Corey Hochachka); © Detlev van Ravensway/Science Photo Library **cover background**; © ESA/NASA/SOHO **08-09**; © Gavin Hellier/Robert Harding **16-17**; © Mark Garlick/Science Photo Library **27**; © NASA **cover, 22, 31**; © NASA Goddard Space Flight Center (NASA-GSFC) **02-03**; © NASA Jet Propulsion Laboratory (NASA-JPL) **13, 14-15, 26**; © NASA/JPL-Caltech **24-25 background;** © NASA/JPL-Caltech/Cornell **20-21**; © NASA/JPL-Caltech/L. Allen (Harvard-Smithsonian CfA) **06-07**; © NASA/JPL/Cornell University **23**; © NASA/JPL/DLR **23**; © NASA/JPL/Space Science Institute cover, **24-25**; © Roger Ressmeyer/CORBIS **01**.

Every effort has been made to trace and acknowledge ownership of copyright. If any rights have been omitted, the publishers offer to rectify this in any subsequent editions following notification.

First published in 2010 by Usborne Publishing Ltd., Usborne House, 83-85 Saffron Hill, London EC1N 8RT, England. www.usborne.com Copyright © 2010 Usborne Publishing Ltd. The name Usborne and the devices ♛ are Trade Marks of Usborne Publishing Ltd. All rights reserved. No part of this publication may be reproduced, stored in a retrieval system, or transmitted in any form or by any means, electronic, mechanical, photocopying, recording or otherwise without the prior permission of the publisher. First published in America 2010. UE.

VOLCANOES

Stephanie Turnbull
Designed by Nancy Leschnikoff
Illustrated by Andy Tudor

Volcano consultant: Professor Gillian Foulger,
Department of Earth Sciences, University of Durham
Reading consultant: Alison Kelly, Roehampton University
Additional illustrations by Tim Haggerty

Contents

- 3 Exploding Earth
- 4 A volcano forms
- 6 Fiery fountains
- 8 Big blasts
- 10 Red-hot rivers
- 12 Deadly clouds
- 14 Undersea eruptions
- 16 Hot water
- 18 Black smokers
- 20 Great geysers
- 22 Dead or alive?
- 24 Violent Vesuvius
- 26 American eruption
- 28 Volcano experts
- 30 Glossary of volcano words
- 31 Websites to visit
- 32 Index

Exploding Earth

There are thousands of volcanoes around the world. Some spray red-hot melted rock called lava. Others blast out clouds of ash.

This is Mount Etna on Sicily shooting out lava.

A volcano forms

The Earth has an outer shell called the crust. Underneath this is a thick layer of hot rock called the mantle.

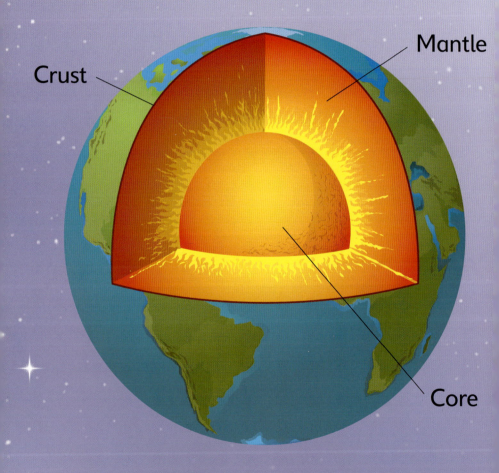

Crust

Mantle

Core

The middle of the Earth is called the core. It is made of extremely hot metal.

There are cracks in the crust. Hot rock melts and pushes up into the cracks.

The melted rock builds up and bursts out as lava. This is called an eruption.

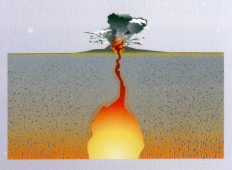

The lava hardens into rock. Layers of lava build up after many eruptions.

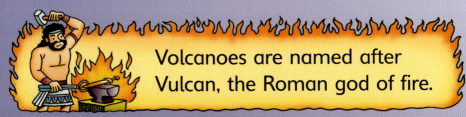

Volcanoes are named after Vulcan, the Roman god of fire.

Fiery fountains

Some lava is runny, so gas inside it bubbles out easily. This creates gentle eruptions.

This is Piton de la Fournaise, on the island of Réunion. Runny lava sprays out of it like a fountain.

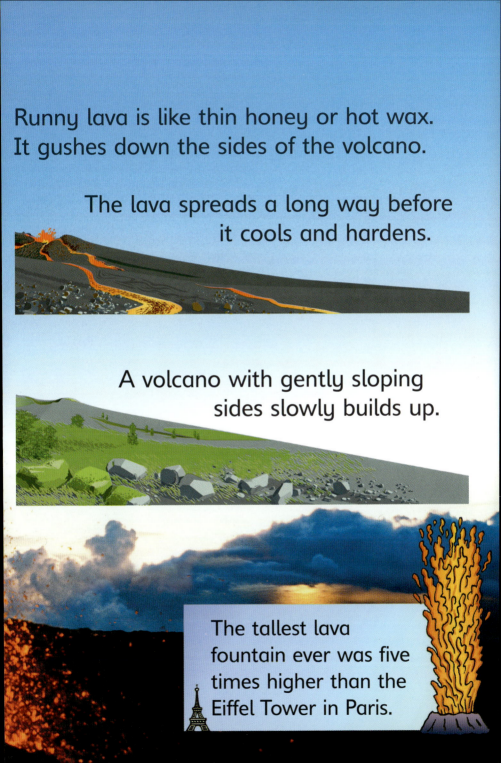

Runny lava is like thin honey or hot wax. It gushes down the sides of the volcano.

The lava spreads a long way before it cools and hardens.

A volcano with gently sloping sides slowly builds up.

The tallest lava fountain ever was five times higher than the Eiffel Tower in Paris.

Big blasts

Some volcanoes have thick lava that is full of gas bubbles. The gas makes lava burst out in a violent eruption.

Clouds of ash and big lumps of lava blast into the air.

Some lumps of lava are jagged rocks called blocks.

Other lumps cool into long, twisted shapes called bombs.

Some blocks of lava are as big as trucks.

Red-hot rivers

Lava that flows from an erupting volcano is much, much hotter than boiling water.

This glowing lava river sets fire to all the trees, plants and buildings it reaches.

Thick lava moves slowly, which gives people and animals time to escape.

Thick lava breaks into rough chunks as it cools down.

Runny lava sets into smooth, swirly shapes instead.

Deadly clouds

Violent eruptions throw out thick clouds of ash, rocks and gas. These clouds sweep down the volcano's slopes.

This terrifying ash cloud came from Mount Pinatubo in the Philippines in 1991. It covered the land all around with a thick blanket of ash.

Sometimes snow and ice on top of high volcanoes melt and mix with the hot ash.

The muddy mixture gushes down the volcano like a river of hot, wet concrete.

Clouds of ash, rocks and gas move faster than a racing car.

Undersea eruptions

Many volcanoes form under the sea. They erupt gently and lava cools quickly in the water.

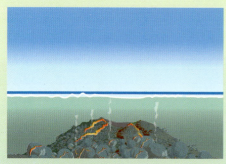

1. An underwater volcano grows taller as it keeps erupting.

2. When it reaches the water's surface, clouds of steam rise.

3. Soon the top of the volcano sticks up out of the sea.

4. The lava keeps building up and forms an island.

This photograph taken from space shows the island of Hawaii.

Hawaii was formed by underwater volcanoes.

The dark area in the middle of the island is Mauna Loa, the world's biggest volcano.

Underwater lava can harden into round rocks called pillow lava.

Hot water

The melted rock underneath a volcano heats up the ground around it.

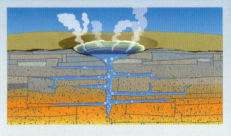

The hot ground also heats up any rain that soaks into it.

Heated water bubbles out and forms a hot spring.

In Iceland, hot spring water is used in swimming pools.

These snow monkeys are keeping warm in a steaming hot spring. The spring is high in the mountains of Japan and is heated by the Shiga Kogen volcano.

Black smokers

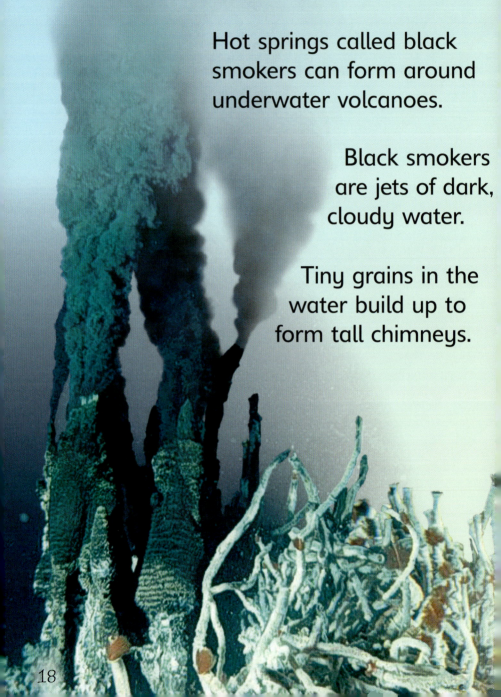

Hot springs called black smokers can form around underwater volcanoes.

Black smokers are jets of dark, cloudy water.

Tiny grains in the water build up to form tall chimneys.

Tubeworms and shrimps feed on the cloudy water around black smokers.

Crabs and long fish called eelpouts also live there, eating smaller animals.

Sometimes a deep sea octopus visits black smokers to search for food.

> Some springs blow out pale clouds of water. They are called white smokers.

Great geysers

Sometimes water heated by a volcano shoots out of the ground with a cloud of steam. This is called a geyser.

Here you can see Old Faithful Geyser in Yellowstone National Park, USA.

Boiling water blasts out of the ground every hour.

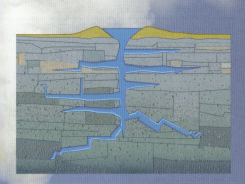
1. Rainwater gets trapped in lots of tiny cracks in the ground.

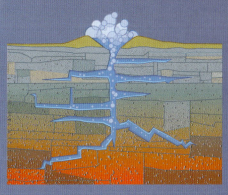
2. Hot volcanic rock heats the water until it fizzes and boils.

3. The boiling water bursts out into the air with a whoosh.

4. It soaks back into the cracks and starts to heat up again.

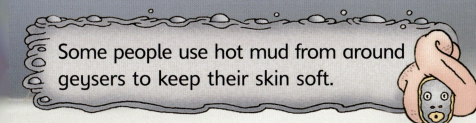
Some people use hot mud from around geysers to keep their skin soft.

Dead or alive?

Volcanoes that are erupting or could erupt in the future are alive. Ones that will never erupt again are dead or extinct.

This is Mount Popa, an extinct volcano in Burma. A temple stands on the top.

A volcano can become extinct if hard lava plugs its main tube or vent.

Over many years the volcano's sides wear away, leaving the lava plug.

Some volcanoes don't erupt for thousands of years, but they are not dead – only sleeping.

Violent Vesuvius

One of the worst eruptions ever was that of Mount Vesuvius in Italy, 2,000 years ago.

Ash and rocks from the volcano rained down on a nearby town called Pompeii.

Some people hurried away from the town, but others hid in their homes instead.

Later that day, Pompeii was buried in a river of mud and ash that set hard, like cement.

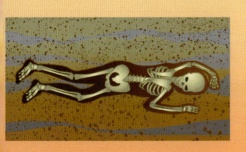

Years later, experts found holes in the rock left by bodies that rotted away.

They filled the holes with plaster, then cut away the rock to see the body shapes.

This is a plaster model of a man who was choked to death by ash.

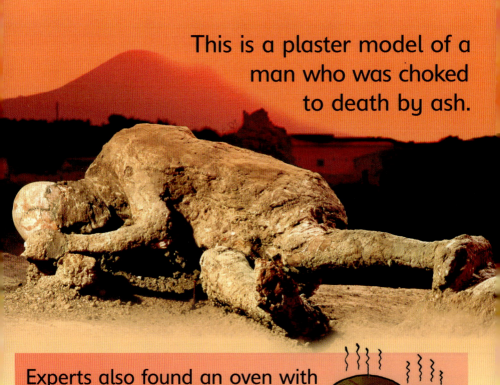

Experts also found an oven with ancient loaves of bread inside.

American eruption

In 1980, the high, snow-covered peak of Mount St. Helens in the USA was blasted away in an enormous eruption.

This is what Mount St. Helens looked like in the years before it erupted.

Then one side of the volcano began to swell up and the ground shook.

Suddenly the volcano's side exploded in a cloud of ash and rocks.

Many small animals escaped the eruption by hiding underground.

This is how Mount St. Helens looked after the eruption. Part of the volcano was gone, and the land around was destroyed.

The volcano began rumbling again in 2004. Another eruption may be on the way.

Volcano experts

Volcanologists are people who study volcanoes and predict when they will erupt.

This volcanologist is using a machine that senses changes in ground level.

A bulge on a volcano's slope could mean melted rock is pushing up inside.

A volcano may give off lots of gas before it erupts, so experts take gas samples.

The ground may also shake before an eruption. A machine records this shaking.

Photographs taken by satellites in space show any changes in the volcano's shape.

Some people think that animals can sense when a volcano is about to erupt.

Glossary of volcano words

Here are some of the words in this book you might not know. This page tells you what they mean.

 lava - melted rock that has erupted from a volcano.

 spring - water that flows out of the ground.

 tubeworm - a long, red-tipped worm that attaches itself to the sea floor.

 geyser - a spring that shoots a jet of steaming hot water out of the ground.

 extinct - dead. An extinct volcano is one that will never erupt again.

 volcanologist - a scientist who studies volcanoes.

 satellite - a machine in space that takes pictures of the Earth's surface.

Websites to visit

You can visit exciting websites to find out more about volcanoes.

To visit these websites, go to the Usborne Quicklinks Website at **www.usborne-quicklinks.com** Read the internet safety guidelines, and then type the keywords "**beginners volcanoes**".

The websites are regularly reviewed and the links in Usborne Quicklinks are updated. However, Usborne Publishing is not responsible, and does not accept liability, for the content or availability of any website other than its own. We recommend that children are supervised while on the internet.

This is Mount Etna, the largest volcano in Europe. It has small eruptions every few months, and big eruptions every few years.

Index

ash, 3, 8, 12, 13, 24, 25, 26
black smokers, 18, 19
crabs, 19
Earth's layers, 4, 5
eelpouts, 19
extinct volcanoes, 22, 23, 30
gas, 6, 8, 12, 13, 29
geysers, 20, 21, 30
Hawaii, 15
hot springs, 16, 17, 18, 19, 30
lava, 3, 5, 6, 7, 8, 9, 10, 11, 14, 15, 23, 30
Mauna Loa, 15
Mount Etna, 2-3, 31
Mount Pinatubo, 12-13
Mount Popa, 22-23
Mount St. Helens, 26, 27
Mount Vesuvius, 24, 25
octopus, 19
Old Faithful Geyser, 20-21
Piton de la Fournaise, 6-7
Pompeii, 24, 25
satellites, 29, 30
Shiga Kogen, 17
shrimps, 19
tubeworms, 19, 30
underwater volcanoes, 14, 15, 18
volcanic islands, 14, 15
volcanologists, 28, 29, 30
Vulcan, 5

Acknowledgements

Photographic manipulation by Mike Wheatley, Nick Wakeford and John Russell
With thanks to Rosie Dickins and Catriona Clarke

Photo credits

The publishers are grateful to the following for permission to reproduce material:
© Age Fotostock/Powerstock 6-7; © Corbis 12-13 (Alberto Garcia), 22-23 (Christophe Loviny), 25 (Roger Ressmeyer); © Getty Images Cover (Ezio Geneletti), 1 (Richard A Cooke III), 31 (Art Wolfe); © Mauritius/Powerstock 8-9; © NASA/Science Photo Library 15; © National Geographic/Getty Images 20-21 (Norbert Rosing); © PhotoLink/Getty Images 27; © Reuters/Corbis 10-11 (Tony Gentile); © Science Photo Library 16-17 (Akira Uchiyama); © Still Pictures 2-3 (Otto Hahn); © University of Victoria 18 (Dr Verena Tunnicliffe); © USGS 28-29 (Mike Poland).

Every effort has been made to trace and acknowledge ownership of copyright. If any rights have been omitted, the publishers offer to rectify this in any subsequent editions following notification.

First published in 2005 by Usborne Publishing Ltd., Usborne House, 83-85 Saffron Hill, London EC1N 8RT, England. www.usborne.com Copyright © 2007, 2005 Usborne Publishing Ltd. The name Usborne and the devices ☿ ♀ are Trade Marks of Usborne Publishing Ltd. All rights reserved. No part of this publication may be reproduced, stored in a retrieval system, or transmitted in any form or by any means, electronic, mechanical, photocopying, recording or otherwise without the prior permission of the publisher.
First published in America 2006. U.E. Printed in China.

Sun, Moon and Stars

Stephanie Turnbull

Designed by Zöe Wray

Illustrated by Kuo Kang Chen and Uwe Mayer

Space consultant: Stuart Atkinson

Reading consultant: Alison Kelly, Roehampton University

Contents

3	The night sky	20	Vanishing trick
4	Out in space	22	Stars
6	The Sun	24	Star groups
8	Earth and Sun	26	Shooting stars
10	Nearby planets	28	Space watch
12	Faraway planets	30	Glossary of space words
14	The Moon		
16	A rocky desert	31	Websites to visit
18	Moon missions	32	Index

The night sky

When you look at the night sky, you can see shining stars, far away in space.

You might be able to spot the Moon too.

Everything you can see is only a tiny part of space.

The Moon looks small, but it would take about four days to drive all the way around it.

Out in space

Our planet Earth is a lump of rock in space. It is one of a group of nine planets.

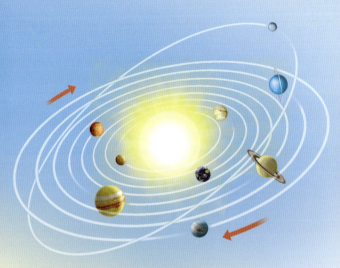

Each planet goes around the Sun on its own invisible path.

The Sun and the planets are called the Solar System.

Mars

Earth

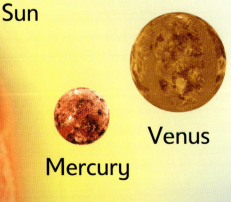

Sun

Venus

Mercury

Experts used to think that Pluto was a planet, but now they've changed their minds and call it a dwarf planet.

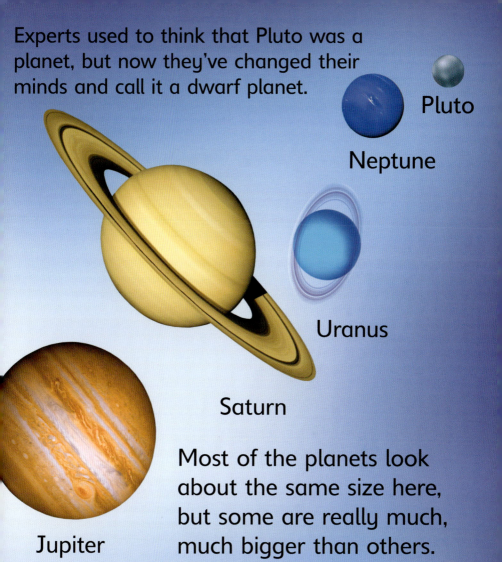

Pluto

Neptune

Uranus

Saturn

Jupiter

Most of the planets look about the same size here, but some are really much, much bigger than others.

Saturn is so far away from Earth that it took seven years for a spacecraft to reach it.

The Sun

The Sun is a star. It is the closest star to Earth, so it looks bigger than other stars.

The Sun was formed by thick clouds of dust and gas.

It became a glowing ball of gas that is hottest in the middle.

The surface of the Sun bubbles and boils.

Sunspot —

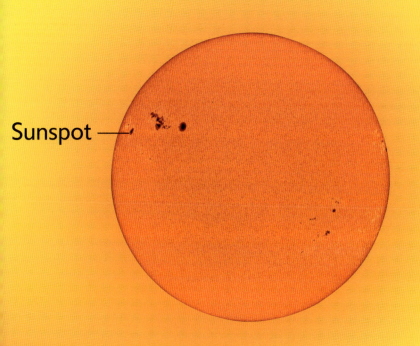

The Sun has dark areas called sunspots. They are cooler than the rest of the Sun.

Never look straight at the Sun. Its strong light can hurt your eyes.

Earth and Sun

Earth turns as it moves around the Sun.

The parts of Earth facing the Sun have day. Parts that light doesn't reach have night. As Earth turns, different parts have day or night.

When it gets dark where you live, it is just getting light on the other side of Earth.

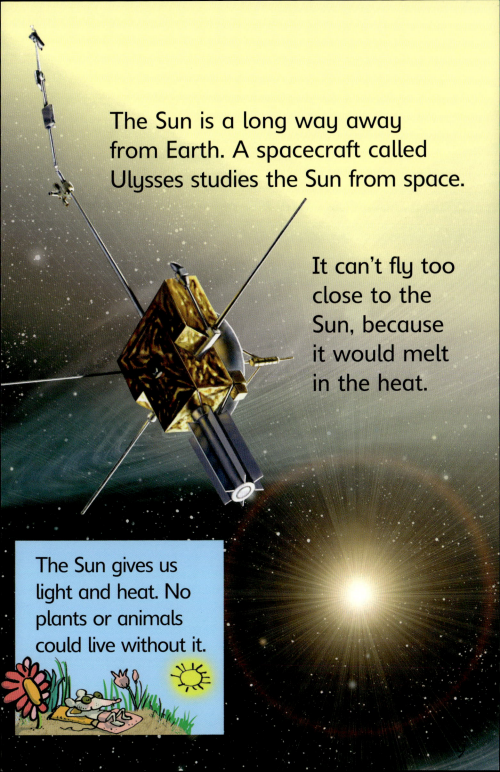

The Sun is a long way away from Earth. A spacecraft called Ulysses studies the Sun from space.

It can't fly too close to the Sun, because it would melt in the heat.

The Sun gives us light and heat. No plants or animals could live without it.

Nearby planets

The four planets closest to the Sun are Mercury, Venus, Earth and Mars.

They are all rocky planets, but Earth is the only one that plants and animals live on.

This is Venus. It has high mountains and volcanoes. The planet's air is poisonous.

A few years ago, a small spacecraft was sent to Mars.

The spacecraft opened up and a robot car drove out.

The car was about the size of a skateboard. Scientists on Earth used computers to make it move and take photos.

Mercury is so close to the Sun that the land is hotter than boiling water.

Faraway planets

Jupiter, Saturn, Uranus and Neptune are far away from the Sun. They are very cold places.

Jupiter is the biggest planet in the Solar System.

This red spot on Jupiter is a storm that is about twice the size of Earth.

Saturn has bright rings around it.

From far away, Saturn's rings look like solid hoops.

In fact each ring is made up of dust, rocks and ice.

The surface of dwarf planet Pluto is frozen, like a huge skating rink.

The Moon

The Moon is a ball of rock that goes around and around the Earth.

As the Moon moves, the Sun lights up different parts of it. This is why the Moon seems to change shape in the night sky.

When the Sun shines behind the Moon, you can't see its light side. It is called a New Moon.

Sometimes you can only see part of the Moon. This is called a Crescent Moon.

When the Sun lights up the whole side of the Moon, you can see a Full Moon.

Other planets have moons too. Jupiter has more than 40 moons.

A rocky desert

The Moon is a dry, dusty place. It has no air or water, so nothing lives there.

The Moon's surface is rocky and hilly. It is covered in giant holes called craters.

Crater

Many of the Moon's craters are so big that whole cities could fit inside them.

There are lots of rocks drifting in space.

Sometimes a rock crashes into the Moon.

The rock explodes and dust flies everywhere.

It makes a deep, bowl-shaped crater.

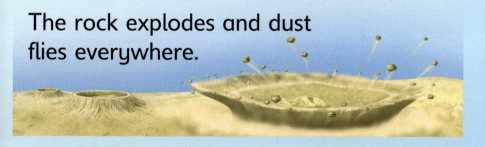

Moon missions

The Moon is the only place in space where people have landed. This is how astronauts got there.

1. A rocket blasted off into space, with astronauts inside.

2. Parts of the rocket fell away, leaving a small spacecraft.

3. A lunar module came out and landed on the Moon.

4. Astronauts climbed down the ladder onto the Moon's surface.

Astronauts explored the Moon in an electric car. They collected rocks to bring back.

This is a piece of rock from the Moon.

In the future, scientists might build special hotels on the Moon for people to stay in.

Vanishing trick

Sometimes the Moon moves in front of the Sun and blocks out the Sun's light. This is called a solar eclipse.

This black circle is the Moon, covering the Sun. Gases from the Sun glow around the edges.

At the start of an eclipse, the Sun looks as if it has a bite taken out of it.

As the Moon covers more of the Sun, the sky gets darker and it feels colder.

The Moon covers the Sun completely for a short time.

During an eclipse, many animals think it must be night, so they get ready to sleep.

Stars

Stars are glowing balls of gas, like the Sun.

The bright star in this photo is much bigger than the Sun, but it looks small because it is so far away.

Some stars slowly get bigger and duller over many years.

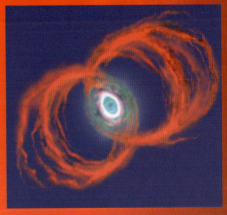

They puff off layers of gas and slowly fade away.

Many stars move around in pairs. They are called double stars.

Some big stars explode. This cloud of gas is all that's left of an exploded star.

Star groups

Stars can be joined up to make patterns.

This pattern of stars is called the Great Dog.

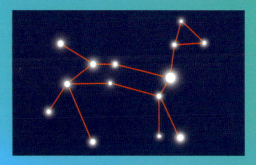

If lines join the stars, you can see a dog shape.

A group of billions of stars is called a galaxy. One galaxy is called the Whirlpool because of its swirling shape.

The Whirlpool galaxy

Most galaxies are spiral or oval shapes. One galaxy looks like a wheel.

Shooting stars

A shooting star is not really a star. It is a small, hot piece of space rock.

Shooting stars are also known as meteors. They look like stars falling out of the sky.

Often lots of space rocks fall at once. This is called a meteor shower.

Space rocks heat up if they come too near Earth.

They burn away, leaving a trail of light behind them.

Some rocks are too big to burn up, so they hit Earth. This huge crater was made by a rock that fell in Arizona, U.S.A.

Space watch

People use telescopes to look at space. They make things look bigger and clearer.

This huge telescope floats around Earth. It takes photos and sends them back to Earth.

A spacecraft took the telescope into space.

A robot arm lifted the telescope out.

At first the telescope didn't work properly. Astronauts had to go into space to fix it.

You can see faraway planets, stars and whole galaxies through powerful telescopes.

Glossary of space words

Here are some of the words in this book you might not know. This page tells you what they mean.

 planet - a huge round object in space. Earth is a planet.

 Solar System - the Sun and the nine planets that go around it.

 crater - a hole on the Moon or a planet, made by a space rock hitting it

 astronaut - a person who is specially trained to travel into space.

 lunar module - a small spacecraft that landed on the Moon.

 galaxy - a group of billions of stars. There are millions of galaxies in space

 telescope - something that makes things far away look bigger and closer

Websites to visit

You can visit exciting websites to find out more about sun, moon and stars.

To visit these websites, go to the Usborne Quicklinks website at **www.usborne.com/quicklinks** Read the internet safety guidelines, and then type the keywords "**beginners sun**".

The websites are regularly reviewed and the links in Usborne Quicklinks are updated. However, Usborne Publishing is not responsible, and does not accept liability, for the content or availability of any website other than its own. We recommend that children are supervised while on the internet.

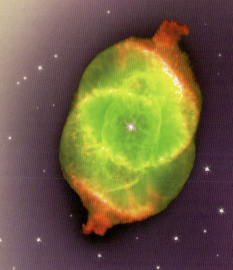

This is a photo of the Cat's Eye Nebula. It was taken through a powerful telescope.

Index

astronauts, 18, 19, 29, 30
craters, 16, 17, 27, 30
Earth, 4, 5, 6, 8, 9, 10, 28
galaxies, 24-25, 30
Jupiter, 5, 12, 15
lunar module, 18, 30
Mars, 4, 10, 11
Mercury, 4, 10, 11
meteors, 26-27
Moon, 3, 14-15, 16-17, 18-19, 20, 21
Neptune, 5, 12
planets, 4-5, 10-11, 12-13, 30
Pluto, 5, 12, 13
Saturn, 5, 12, 13
shooting stars, 26-27
solar eclipse, 20-21
Solar System, 4-5, 12, 30
spacecraft, 5, 9, 11, 18, 28
space rocks, 17, 26, 27
stars, 3, 6, 22-23, 24-25
Sun, 4, 6-7, 8, 9, 10, 14, 15, 20, 21, 22
telescopes, 28-29, 30
Ulysses, 9
Uranus, 5, 12
Venus, 4, 10

Acknowledgements

Cover design: Nicola Butler
Photographic manipulation by Emma Julings and John Russell

Photo credits

The publishers are grateful to the following for permission to reproduce material:
© **Alamy** 2-3 (Doug Steley), 16 (Pictor International); © **Corbis** 1 (Myron Jay Dorf), 8 (Roger Ressmeyer), 27 (Charles & Josette Lenars); © **David A. Hardy** 9 (astroart.org); © **Digital Vision** Cover (Earth); © **ESO/NASA** 22-23, 24-25, 30 (galaxy); © **NASA** Cover (Moon), 4-5, 6-7, 14, 15, 19, 28, 29, 31; © **Science Photo Library** 10 (David P. Anderson, SMU/NASA), 11 & 12 (NASA), 13, 20 (Chris Butler)

Every effort has been made to trace and acknowledge ownership of copyright. If any rights have been omitted, the publishers offer to rectify this in any subsequent editions following notification.

First published in 2003 by Usborne Publishing Ltd., Usborne House, 83-85 Saffron Hill, London EC1N 8RT, England. www.usborne.com Copyright © 2007, 2003 Usborne Publishing Ltd. The name Usborne and the devices ⚛ are Trade Marks of Usborne Publishing Ltd. All rights reserved. No part of this publication may be reproduced, stored in a retrieval system, or transmitted in any form or by any means, electronic, mechanical, photocopying, recording or otherwise without the prior permission of the publisher.
First published in America 2003. U.E. Printed in China.

Weather

Catriona Clarke
Designed by Andrea Slane
Illustrated by Kuo Kang Chen

Additional illustrations by Tim Haggerty
Weather consultant: Dr. Roger Trend, University of Exeter
Reading consultant: Alison Kelly, Roehampton University

Contents

- 3   Rain or shine
- 4   What is weather?
- 6   Water on the move
- 8   Clouding over
- 10   Icy crystals
- 12   Electric skies
- 14   Great balls of ice
- 16   Wild wind
- 18   Terrible twisters
- 20   Weather scientists
- 22   Animal magic
- 24   Hot and cold
- 26   Weird weather
- 28   Heating up?
- 30   Glossary of weather words
- 31   Websites to visit
- 32   Index

Rain or shine

The weather can be sunny, rainy, windy or snowy. Every kind of weather is happening somewhere in the world right now.

This is a snowstorm in New York, USA.

What is weather?

The weather is caused by three main things: heat, water and air.

The Sun gives out heat which warms the Earth.

Water makes clouds and rain. It also makes fog, hail and snow.

Air is always moving around. This is what makes the wind blow.

The Earth is wrapped in a thick blanket of air called the atmosphere. This is where weather happens.

From space, the atmosphere looks like a hazy blue ring around the Earth. The white swirls are clouds.

Water on the move

Water is always moving between the sea, the air and the land. This is called the water cycle.

1. The Sun warms the water in the sea and turns it into an invisible gas.

2. The gas rises and turns into tiny droplets of water, making clouds.

The rain that falls on you may have fallen on a dinosaur millions of years ago.

3. The tiny droplets bump into each other and join together to make bigger drops.

4. When the drops of water become heavy enough they fall as rain.

5. Rivers carry the rainwater back to the sea. The water cycle begins again.

Clouding over

Different types of clouds mean there will be different kinds of weather.

Puffy white cumulus clouds usually mean that good weather is coming.

Stratus clouds cover the sky. This means that there might be fog or drizzle.

Wispy cirrus clouds high in the sky mean rain or snow may be coming later.

A big cumulonimbus cloud means that there may be a thunderstorm.

When tiny water droplets form close to the ground, this is called fog or mist.

This is the Golden Gate Bridge in California, USA. It is foggy there most of the time.

Icy crystals

When the air is very cold, the water in clouds freezes to make tiny ice crystals called snowflakes.

Most snowflakes have six points.

No two snowflakes are ever exactly the same shape.

This is what snowflakes look like when they are put under a microscope.

Icicles form in snowy weather when the Sun shines onto snow on roofs or trees.

The snow melts. Water drips down into the cold shade, where it freezes.

More water slowly drips down and freezes, forming lots of icy 'fingers'.

Electric skies

Thunderstorms happen when a cumulonimbus cloud forms in the sky.

Strong winds inside the cloud swirl rain, snow and hailstones up and down.

This makes electricity build up. It escapes down to the ground as flashes of lightning.

Lightning sometimes hits trees and buildings on its way from the cloud to the ground.

Thunder is the sound that lightning makes when it heats up the air around it.

This type of lightning is called forked lightning.

You always see lightning before you hear thunder, because light travels faster than sound.

Great balls of ice

Hail forms inside giant thunderclouds, so you often get hailstorms at the same time as thunder and lightning.

1. Water droplets get blown up to the top of the cloud by gusts of air.

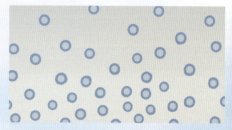

2. The droplets freeze. They drop down and a layer of water forms around them.

3. The hail is blown up to the top of the cloud again and the layer of water freezes.

4. This happens again and again until the hail gets too heavy and falls from the sky.

If a hailstone is cut in half, its layers look a bit like those in an onion.

This is the biggest hailstone ever. It fell in Nebraska, USA in 2003.

It is shown here at just over half its actual size.

Wild wind

Wind is moving air. It happens when hot air rises and cold air rushes in to take its place.

The strength of the wind is measured on a scale from 1 to 12.

A force 2 breeze dries the clothes on a clothesline.

A force 5 wind blows the leaves from the trees.

A force 9 wind is a severe gale. It can blow tiles from roofs.

A force 12 wind is a hurricane. It can destroy houses.

A hurricane begins when hot air rises quickly over the sea and starts to spin. This causes a violent storm with heavy rain.

When a hurricane reaches land, huge waves and strong winds batter the coast.

The Ancient Greeks believed that the wind was the breath of the Gods.

Terrible twisters

Tornadoes are violent, whirling winds. They are sometimes called twisters.

A tornado is like a giant vacuum cleaner. It sucks things up from the ground.

1. The air inside a thundercloud slowly begins to spin around and around.

2. The air spins faster and faster. The cloud begins to change shape.

3. Warm air is sucked up into the cloud. It becomes shaped like a funnel.

4. The cloud touches the ground and as it moves, it destroys everything in its path.

Twisters can sometimes suck fish and frogs out of ponds.

Weather scientists

Scientists measure the weather and then tell us what they think the weather will be like.

Wind speed and rain are measured at weather stations all over the world.

Special planes fly into clouds to measure how much water is in them.

Satellites in space take pictures of clouds and storms on Earth.

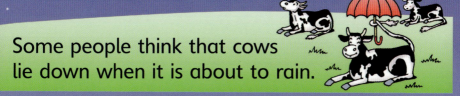

Some people think that cows lie down when it is about to rain.

Weather balloons are sent high into the sky to measure the air temperature.

The scientists put together all this information to make a weather forecast.

The white, swirling cloud below is a hurricane in the Atlantic Ocean.

Animal magic

Weather doesn't just affect people, it affects the way animals behave too.

For example, the fur of a snowshoe hare changes from brown to white for the winter.

The hare can't be spotted in the snow by eagles that hunt it.

Every year some birds fly a very long way to escape the cold winter weather.

Some animals, like dormice, sleep through the long, cold winter. This is called hibernation.

When it gets colder, a dormouse eats lots of fruit and seeds.

It makes a snug nest underground or in a tree and goes to sleep.

Six months later, it wakes up, ready for the summer ahead.

Hot and cold

Some places have such extreme weather that not many people or animals live there.

The Sahara Desert in Africa is one of the hottest and driest places on Earth.

Camels can live here because they can survive without water for a long time.

Under the hot sun, desert rocks become so hot that you could fry an egg on them!

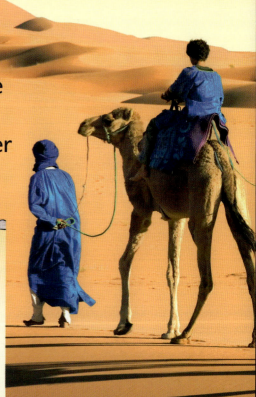

Antarctica is the coldest place in the world.

Penguins are one of the few animals that are able to live there.

They huddle close together to keep warm in the winter.

Weird weather

In some parts of the world the weather makes odd things happen.

Some people think that strange clouds like this one look like spaceships.

It is called a lenticular cloud. They usually form near mountains.

Red raindrops sometimes fall from the sky.

Winds pick up red sand from African deserts and carry it across the sea.

The sand mixes with droplets of water in the clouds to make the red rain.

A hailstone with a turtle inside once fell from a thundercloud in Mississippi, USA!

Heating up?

Many scientists think that the Earth's atmosphere is slowly getting warmer.

The air in the atmosphere acts like a blanket to keep the Earth warm.

When fuels like oil and coal are burned, lots of gases are released into the air.

The atmosphere is getting warmer because the gases trap heat from the Sun.

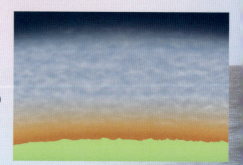

Animals add to the gases released into the air.

If the Earth gets warmer, the weather will change. In cold places, ice and snow would melt and could cause massive floods.

Hundreds of years from now, all this ice might have melted.

Glossary of weather words

Here are some of the words in this book you might not know. This page tells you what they mean.

 droplet - a tiny drop of water. Water droplets join together to make clouds.

 ice crystal - a frozen drop of water. Snowflakes are ice crystals.

 lightning - a flash of light from a thundercloud.

 hailstone - a lump of ice formed inside a thundercloud.

 hurricane - a fierce storm. These are also known as typhoons or cyclones.

 weather station - a place where scientists measure the weather.

 weather forecast - a report about what the weather is going to be like.

Websites to visit

You can visit exciting websites to find out more about weather.

To visit these websites, go to the Usborne Quicklinks Website at **www.usborne.com/quicklinks** Read the internet safety guidelines, and then type the keywords "**beginners weather**".

The websites are regularly reviewed and the links in Usborne Quicklinks are updated. However, Usborne Publishing is not responsible, and does not accept liability, for the content or availability of any website other than its own. We recommend that children are supervised while on the internet.

This child is wearing waterproof clothes to keep dry in the rain.

Index

air, 4, 5, 6, 10, 13, 14, 16, 17, 19, 21, 28, 29
animals, 22-23, 24, 25, 27, 29
Antarctica, 25
atmosphere, 5, 28
clouds, 4, 5, 6, 7, 8-9, 10, 12, 14, 19, 20, 21, 26, 27, 30
cold, 10, 11, 16, 23, 25, 29
fog, 4, 8, 9
hail, 4, 12, 14-15, 27, 30
heat, 4, 13, 16, 17, 24-28
hibernation, 23
hurricanes, 16, 17, 21, 30
icicles, 11
lightning, 12-13, 14, 30
people, 24
rain, 4, 7, 9, 12, 17, 20, 21, 27
Sahara Desert, 24
satellites, 20
snow, 3, 4, 9, 10-11, 12, 22, 29
snowflakes, 10-11, 30
sun, 4, 6, 11, 24, 28
thunderstorms, 9, 12-13
tornadoes, 18-19
water cycle, 6-7
weather forecast, 21, 30
weather scientists, 20-21
wind, 4, 12, 16-17, 18, 20

Acknowledgements

Photographic manipulation by Nick Wakeford
With thanks to Stephanie Turnbull

Photo credits

The publishers are grateful to the following for permission to reproduce material:

Cover © Kent Wood/ Science Photo Library; **1** © Digital Archive Japan/Alamy; **2-3** © Jose Luis Pelaez, Inc./CORBIS; **8-9** © Ed Pritchard/Getty Images; **10-11** © Bettman/CORBIS; **13** © A. T. Willett/Alamy; **15** © Quilla Ulmer/Jim Reed Photography/Science Photo Library; **17** © Warren Faidley/CORBIS; **18-19** © Eric Meola/Getty Images; **20-21** © Orbimage/Science Photo Library; **22** © T. Kitchin & V. Hurst/Photoshot; **24-25** © Martin Harvey/Photoshot; **26-27** © Magrath/Folsom/Science Photo Library; **29** © Paul A. Souders/CORBIS; **31** © Christopher Furlong/Getty Images.

Every effort has been made to trace and acknowledge ownership of copyright. If any rights have been omitted, the publishers offer to rectify this in any subsequent editions following notification.

First published in 2006 by Usborne Publishing Ltd., Usborne House, 83-85 Saffron Hill, London EC1N 8RT, England. www.usborne.com Copyright © 2006 Usborne Publishing Ltd. The name Usborne and the devices ⚛ are Trade Marks of Usborne Publishing Ltd. All rights reserved. No part of this publication may be reproduced, stored in a retrieval system, or transmitted in any form or by any means, electronic, mechanical, photocopying, recording or otherwise without the prior permission of the publisher. First published in America 2006. U.E.

Living in space

Katie Daynes
Designed by Zoe Wray

Illustrated by Christyan Fox and Alex Pang

Space consultant: Stuart Atkinson

Reading consultant: Alison Kelly,
Roehampton University

Contents

3   Earth and space
4   Space school
6   Preparing to go
8   Lift off
10 In orbit
12 A home in space
14 The space station
16 Eating and drinking
18 Keeping clean
20 A day in space
22 Spacesuits
24 Going outside
26 Back to Earth
28 Space trips
30 Glossary of space words
31 Web sites to visit
32 Index

Earth and space

The Earth is a big round planet.
This is what it looks like from space.

Astronauts travel into space to live and work.

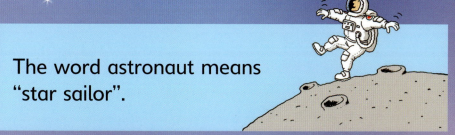

The word astronaut means
"star sailor".

Space school

To become an astronaut, you have to go to space school and learn how to live in space.

On Earth when things jump they go up and then down.

An invisible force called gravity pulls them down.

In space there is very little gravity so everything floats.

Astronauts need lots of training to know what to do when they float in space.

At space school, astronauts learn how to work while floating in water. It feels like working in space.

Astronauts also try out emergency escapes.

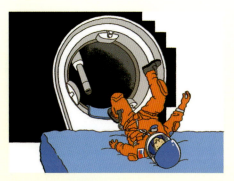

They slide down a pole onto a soft mat.

Preparing to go

Astronauts fly to space in a space shuttle. The shuttle leaves from a launch pad.

The shuttle looks like a plane with a big fuel tank and two white rockets.

Bridge

Fuel tank

Launch pad

  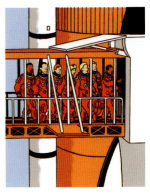

The astronauts put on special orange suits.

They travel to the shuttle in an elevator.

Then they cross a bridge into the shuttle.

The astronauts lie in the nose of the shuttle and wait until it's time to go.

Lift off

The engines start burning fuel from the fuel tank. Then the two rockets light up and the shuttle zooms into space.

3... 2... 1... Lift off!

Nobody is allowed to stand close to the launch pad because it is too dangerous.

After two minutes, the rockets fall into the sea.

After eight minutes, the fuel tank falls away.

The shuttle is now floating in space.

Two flaps open up on the back of the shuttle so it doesn't get too hot inside.

In orbit

The space shuttle goes around the Earth in a big circle. This is known as being in orbit.

It only takes 90 minutes for the shuttle to orbit the Earth.

The middle part of the shuttle is called the payload bay. It carries big objects into space.

The astronauts work, eat and sleep in the nose of the shuttle.

A home in space

Some astronauts stay in space for a long time. They live in a floating home called a space station.

Astronauts are building a big, new space station. This is what it will look like when it's finished.

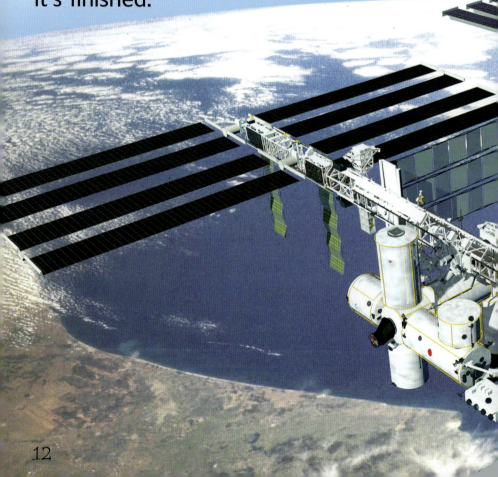

The shuttle travels through space.

It flies close to the space station.

Then it joins onto the space station.

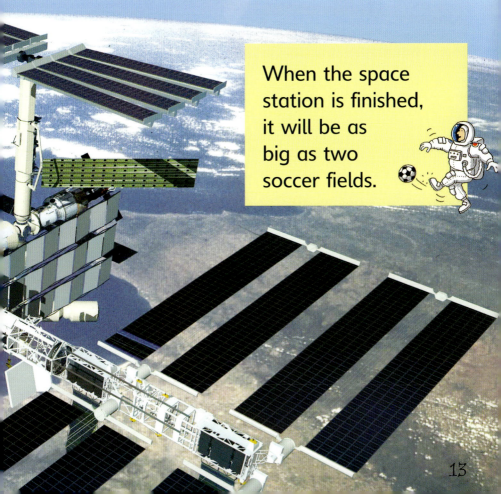

When the space station is finished, it will be as big as two soccer fields.

The space station

The space shuttle carries the parts for the new space station into space.

A robot arm on the shuttle picks a big tube out of the payload bay.

The robot arm then joins the new tube onto the space station.

Some of the tubes are as big as a bus.

Eating and drinking

When astronauts go into space they take their food and drinks with them.

The first meals taken to space didn't look or taste very nice.

Beef with vegetables

Food was dried and sealed up.

Astronauts added warm water...

...which made the food soggy.

Can you see the blob of drink floating to the astronaut's mouth?

Today, most space meals come already prepared in trays. They just need to be heated. Fruit is dried to keep it fresh.

Dried strawberries

The first man to walk on the Moon ate dried ice cream in space.

Keeping clean

It is difficult living in a space station. There is not much room and everything floats.

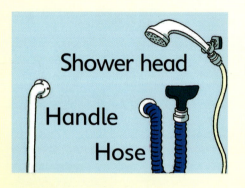

In a space shower the water flows out then floats in blobs.

An astronaut holds onto the handle to keep still while he washes.

After rinsing, he uses a hose to suck up all the water.

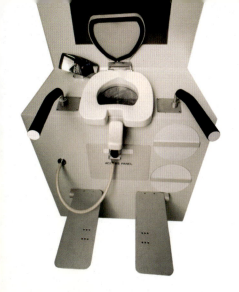 

A space toilet has bars and foot rests to help the astronaut sit down.

An astronaut slides the bars over her legs and turns on the air flow.

Astronauts recycle some water in space and more comes from Earth in tanks like these.

A day in space

Astronauts work in the space station. Some work in a laboratory, like the one below. It's a tube where they can carry out tests.

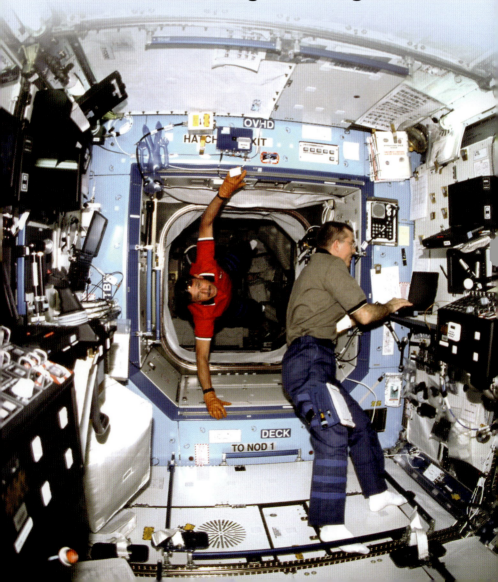

They also fit new parts inside the space station.

They exercise every day to keep fit and healthy.

They sleep in a sleeping bag attached to the wall.

When they're not working, astronauts read, listen to music, or just look at the amazing views of Earth.

Astronauts can talk to people on Earth and send messages by computer.

Spacesuits

When astronauts work outside the space station they have to wear a spacesuit.

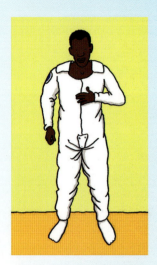  

The first layer keeps them cool or warm.

They add an outer layer for protection.

The helmet and gloves go on last.

Inside their helmets astronauts can drink through a straw and talk to each other.

Straw

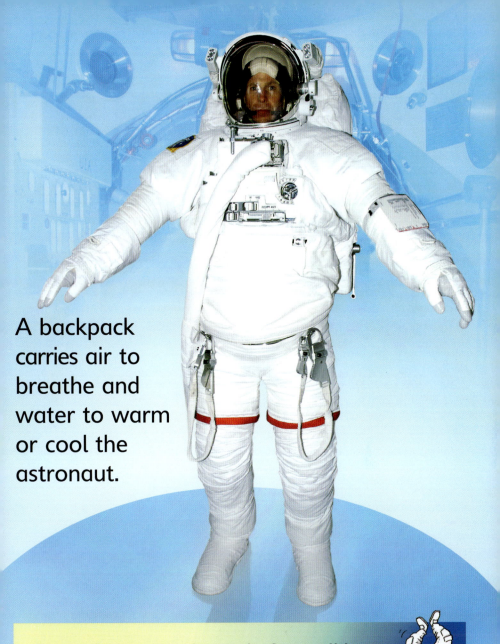

A backpack carries air to breathe and water to warm or cool the astronaut.

Space boots aren't made for walking. The astronauts move around by holding onto things with their hands.

Going outside

Astronauts go out into space through an airlock. It stops air from escaping from the space station.

  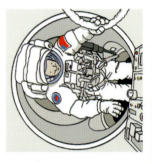

An astronaut goes through the first door.

In the airlock he puts on a spacesuit.

He leaves through the second door.

An astronaut sometimes puts on a jet pack so he can move around outside the space station.

When astronauts work outside it is called spacewalking. This astronaut is spacewalking in the shuttle's payload bay.

One astronaut dropped a glove in space. It is still floating around somewhere.

Back to Earth

After 90 days on the space station the astronauts travel back to Earth.

The shuttle leaves the space station.

It heats up as it drops back through the air.

The shuttle lands on a runway like a plane.

A parachute helps it to slow down.

The longest an astronaut has stayed in space is one year and 72 days.

Space trips

The first trip to space was in 1957.

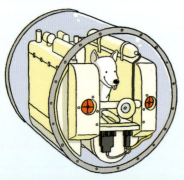

The first living thing to travel from Earth to space was a dog named Laika.

In 1969 astronauts walked on the moon for the first time.

There is no wind or rain on the Moon, so footprints stay for hundreds of years.

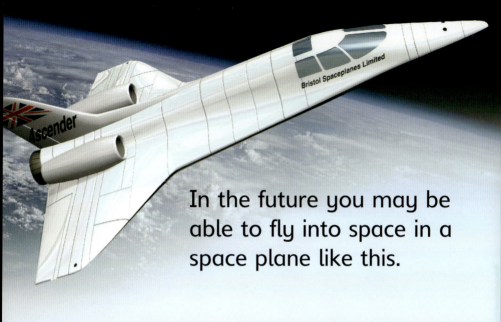

In the future you may be able to fly into space in a space plane like this.

People might also live in space homes like this.

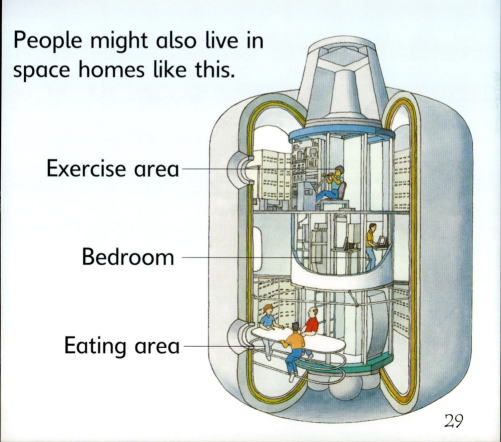

Exercise area

Bedroom

Eating area

Glossary of space words

Here are some of the words in this book you might not know. This page tells you what they mean.

 planet - a huge round object in space. The Earth is a planet.

 gravity - an invisible force that pulls things on Earth down to the ground.

 fuel - something which burns to give the shuttle power to move very fast.

 in orbit - going around a planet in a big circle.

 payload bay - the middle part of the shuttle where big objects are carried.

 laboratory - a place where people carry out tests.

 airlock - a set of doors for getting into and out of a space station or shuttle.

Websites to visit

You can visits exciting websites to find out more about living in space.

To visit these websites, go to the Usborne Quicklinks Website at **www.usborne-quicklinks.com** Read the internet safety guidelines, and then type the keywords "**beginners space**".

The websites are regularly reviewed and the links in Usborne Quicklinks are updated. However, Usborne Publishing in not responsible, and does not accept liability, for the content or availability of any website other than its own. We recommend that children are supervised while on the internet.

The shiny visor on this helmet reflects sunlight to protect the astronaut's eyes.

Index

airlock, 24, 30
bedroom, 15, 29
drink, 16-17, 22
Earth, 3, 4, 11, 12, 19, 21, 26, 28, 30
eating, 11, 15, 16-17, 29
exercise, 21, 29
food, 16-17
fuel tank, 6, 8, 9
gravity, 4, 30
jet pack, 24
laboratory, 20, 30
Moon, 17, 28
orbit, 10, 11, 30
parachute, 27
payload bay, 11, 25, 30
rockets, 6, 8, 9
shower, 15, 18
shuttle, 6, 7, 8, 9, 10, 11, 13, 14, 25, 26, 30
space station, 12-13, 14-15, 18, 20, 22, 24, 26, 30
spacesuits, 22-23, 24
spacewalking, 25
toilet, 15, 19
water, 5, 16, 18, 19, 23

Acknowledgements

Cover design: Nicola Butler

Photo credits

The publishers are grateful to the following for permission to reproduce material:
© **Bristol Spaceplanes** 29, © **Corbis** (Richard T. Nowitz) 4, (Bettmann) 6, (Digital image © 1996 CORBIS; Original image courtesy of NASA/CORBIS) 9, (Bettmann) 16, (Roger Ressmeyer) 19, © **Digital Vision** Cover, 3, 26, © **Genesis Space Photo Library** 7, 19, © **NASA** Cover, 1, 5, 8, 12-13, 19, 20, 21, 23, 24, 25, 26-27, 28, 31

With thanks to
Katie Towers at Buxton Foods Ltd for the space strawberries.

Every effort has been made to trace and acknowledge ownership of copyright. If any rights have been omitted, the publishers offer to rectify this in any subsequent editions following notification.

First published in 2002 by Usborne Publishing Ltd., Usborne House, 83-85 Saffron Hill, London EC1N 8RT, England. www.usborne.com Copyright © 2006, 2002 Usborne Publishing Ltd. The name Usborne and the devices ⓠ ⊕ are Trade Marks of Usborne Publishing Ltd. All rights reserved. No part of this publication may be reproduced, stored in a retrieval system, or transmitted in any form or by any means, electronic, mechanical, photocopying, recording or otherwise without the prior permission of the publisher.
First published in America 2003. U.E. Printed in China.

Planet Earth

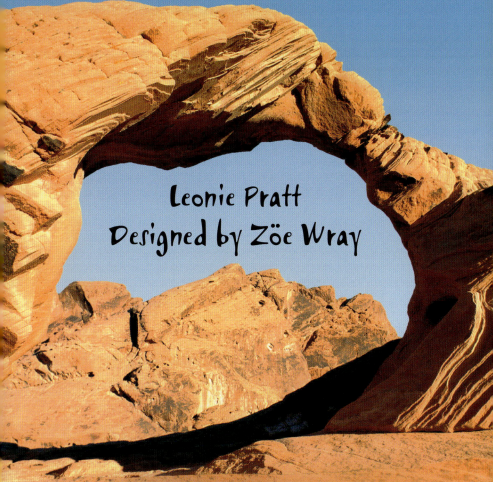

Leonie Pratt

Designed by Zöe Wray

Illustrated by Andy Tudor

Additional illustrations by Tim Haggerty

Planet Earth consultant: Dr. Gillian Foulger, Department of Earth Sciences, Durham University
Reading consultant: Alison Kelly, Roehampton University

Contents

- 3 A place in space
- 4 All about Earth
- 6 Moving Earth
- 8 Mountain high
- 10 Volcanoes
- 12 Rock around the world
- 14 Running rivers
- 16 Wearing away
- 18 Underground caves
- 20 Cold as ice
- 22 Coast
- 24 Deep water
- 26 Dusty deserts
- 28 Extraordinary Earth
- 30 Glossary of Earth words
- 31 Websites to visit
- 32 Index

Neptune

Uranus

Saturn

A place in space

You live on Earth, one of the eight planets that move around the Sun.

Scientists think that Earth is the only planet with anything living on it.

All about Earth

Things can live on Earth because it has the right mixture of heat, air and water.

The Sun keeps the planet warm.

Living things – people, animals and plants – all need air to breathe.

Over half of the Earth is covered in water. All living things need water to stay alive.

The middle of the planet is called the core. It is very, very hot here.

Around the core is the mantle. The rocks here are so hot that they are slightly squishy.

The mantle is covered with a thin layer of solid rock, called the crust.

Moving Earth

The Earth's crust is made up of pieces.

 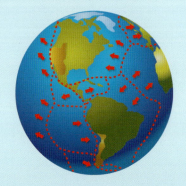

The pieces of crust slot together around the Earth.

Very very slowly, the pieces of crust move around.

The place where the pieces slide past each other is called a fault.

Pieces of crust can move smoothly along a fault, but sometimes they get jammed.

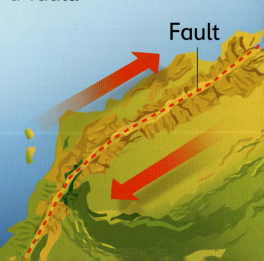

Fault

Jammed pieces can suddenly start to slip past one another. The land above trembles and cracks. This is called an earthquake.

Big earthquakes can destroy buildings and tear up roads.

There are even 'earthquakes' on the moon. These are called moonquakes.

Mountain high

As the crust moves, it slowly pushes some of the land up into tall, rocky mountains.

The mountains in this picture are the Alps, in Europe. It took millions of years for them to get this tall.

Some mountains, such as the Himalayas, are growing taller every year.

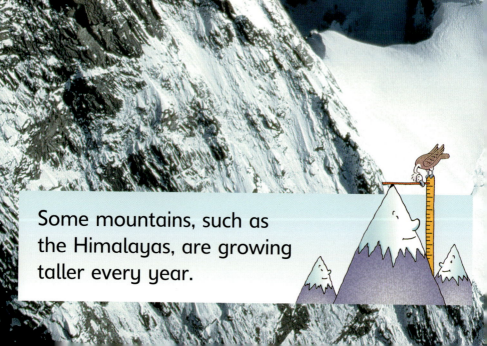

Mountain peaks stay snowy because the air is cold high up... ... so mountain goats need thick coats to keep them warm.

Volcanoes

Hot rock from the mantle can creep up through cracks in the crust and escape onto the land as a volcano.

This is a volcano erupting.

The hot rock that escapes is called lava.

Some people in Hawaii think that the goddess of fire lives in a volcano.

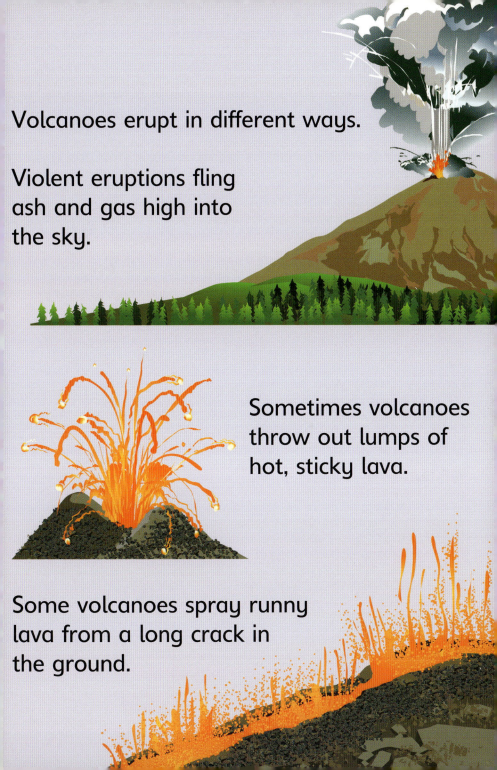

Volcanoes erupt in different ways.

Violent eruptions fling ash and gas high into the sky.

Sometimes volcanoes throw out lumps of hot, sticky lava.

Some volcanoes spray runny lava from a long crack in the ground.

Rock around the world

All the land on Earth is made of rock. There are three main types of rock.

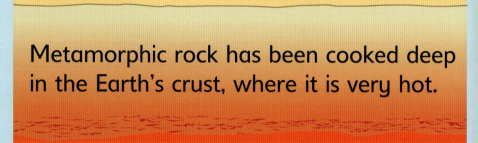

Metamorphic rock has been cooked deep in the Earth's crust, where it is very hot.

Igneous rock forms when lava from a volcano cools in the air and turns hard.

Jewels such as diamonds, rubies and emeralds are found inside rocks.

Sedimentary rock is made from layers of mud or sand pressed together.

The different layers in this rock make it look striped.

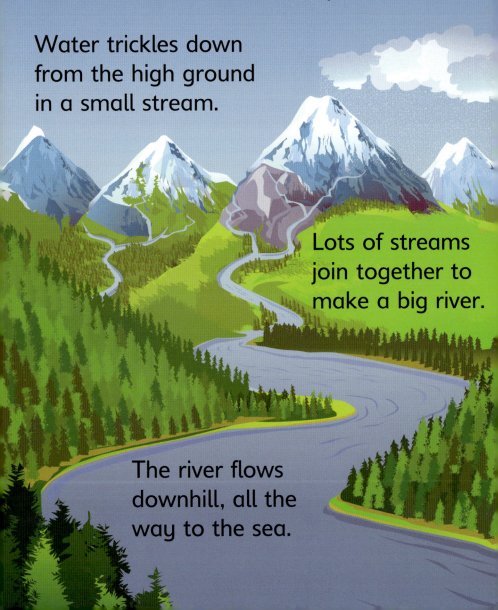

Running rivers

When it rains or snows on the mountains, the hard rock cannot soak up all the water.

Water trickles down from the high ground in a small stream.

Lots of streams join together to make a big river.

The river flows downhill, all the way to the sea.

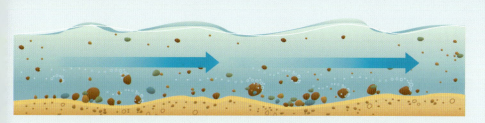

A fast-flowing river picks up lots of stones and pebbles from the riverbed.

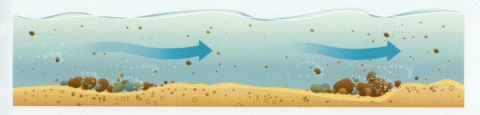

When the river slows down, it drops the heavier stones, but still carries small pebbles.

As the river gets near the sea, it slows down so much that it drops almost everything.

The Nile in Africa is the longest river in the world. It is so big it can even be seen from space.

Wearing away

Rivers change the shape of the land as they flow over it.

A river flows over the land, picking up stones and soil from the ground.

The stones bump along the riverbed, wearing away a groove in the land.

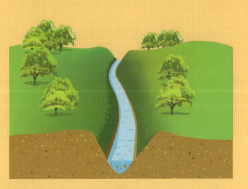

Over many years, the river carves a valley into the ground below.

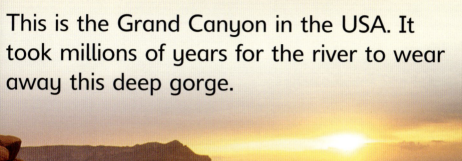

This is the Grand Canyon in the USA. It took millions of years for the river to wear away this deep gorge.

Underground caves

Not all rivers flow over the land – some flow under it. Rivers that flow underground can wear away the rock to make caves.

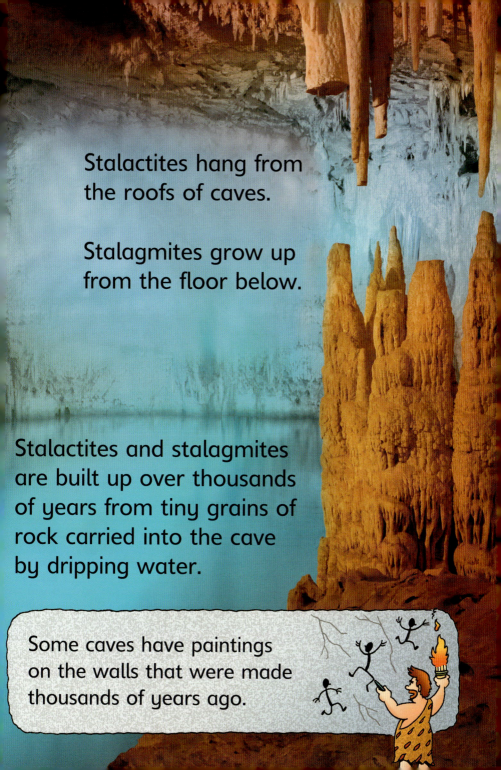

Stalactites hang from the roofs of caves.

Stalagmites grow up from the floor below.

Stalactites and stalagmites are built up over thousands of years from tiny grains of rock carried into the cave by dripping water.

Some caves have paintings on the walls that were made thousands of years ago.

Cold as ice

Some of the Earth's water stays frozen as ice for most of the year.

Antarctica is the coldest place in the world.

The land is covered with snow, and icebergs float in the sea.

1. Ice spreads from the land and floats on the sea.

2. The sea moves up and down, causing the ice to crack.

In Antarctica, it gets so cold in winter that even the sea freezes over.

3. The crack gets bigger until a block of ice breaks off.

4. The block floats away in the sea as an iceberg.

Coast

The coast is where the land meets the sea.

Sand is made from broken up shells and rocks. The sea grinds the pieces into tiny grains, then washes them ashore.

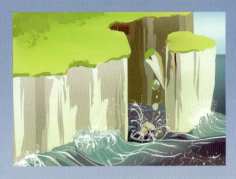

Waves crash against the sides of a cliff, wearing the rock away into an arch.

The top of the arch falls into the water, leaving a stack standing in the sea.

This is a stack.

Some beaches have black sand made from volcanic rock.

Deep water

Oceans and seas cover more than half of the Earth. Many different things live there.

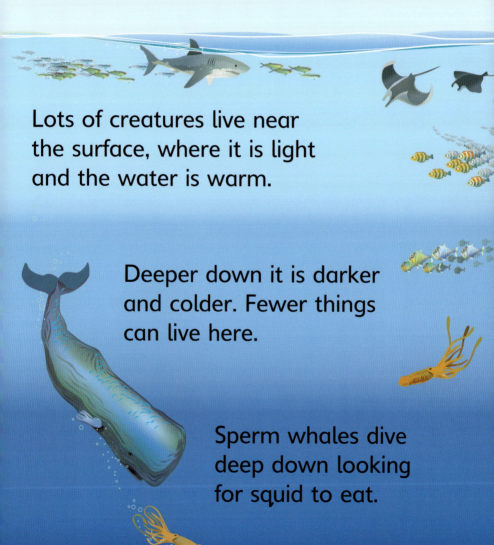

Lots of creatures live near the surface, where it is light and the water is warm.

Deeper down it is darker and colder. Fewer things can live here.

Sperm whales dive deep down looking for squid to eat.

Scientists use submarines like this one to dive deep into the sea and explore the ocean floor.

Some deep sea fish glow in the dark to attract small fish – then they eat them!

Dusty deserts

Deserts are the driest places on Earth. Very little rain falls and the land is dry and dusty.

The Sahara desert in Africa is one of the biggest deserts in the world.

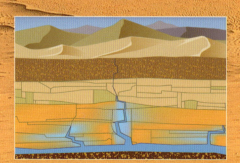

1. Even in the desert, water is trapped in rocks underground.

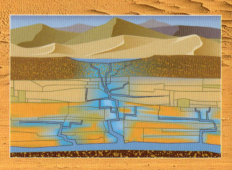

2. Over a long time, the water builds up and forms a pool.

Desert animals stay underground during the hot days and come out at night to find food.

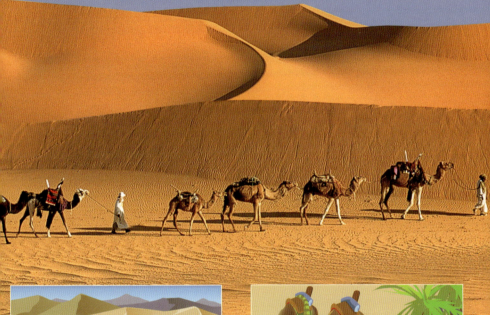

3. Plants grow near the pool. This is called an oasis.

4. People who travel across deserts often stop at an oasis.

Extraordinary Earth

Planet Earth is an amazing place...

Greenland is the largest island in the world.

North America

Angel Falls, Venezuela is the world's tallest waterfall. It is 979m (3,212ft) high.

South America

Some parts of the Atacama desert in Chile, went without rain for 400 years.

Mount Everest is the highest place in the world. It is 8,850m (29,035ft) high.

The deepest part of the Marianas Trench is about 11,000m (36,089ft) underwater.

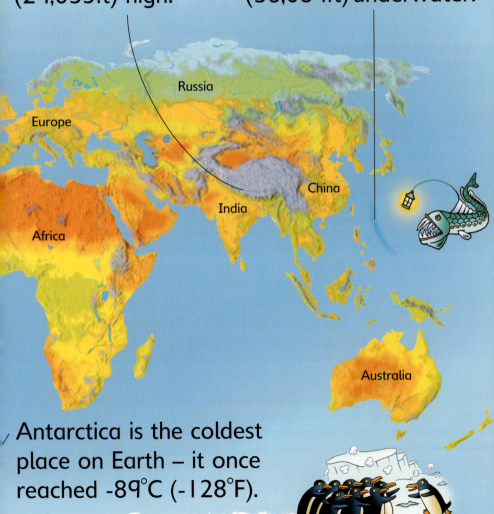

Antarctica is the coldest place on Earth – it once reached -89°C (-128°F).

Glossary of Earth words

Here are some of the words in this book you might not know. This page tells you what they mean.

 fault - the place where two pieces of crust meet.

 eruption - when hot rock escapes onto the land from a volcano.

 lava - red-hot melted rock that has erupted from a volcano.

 gorge - a deep valley, with steep sides that have been carved out by a river.

 iceberg - a big block of ice that floats in the sea. Most of it is underwater.

 desert - a place where there is very little rainfall in a year.

 oasis - a pool in a desert where water has risen up from below the ground.

Websites to visit

You can visit exciting websites to find out more about Planet Earth.

To visit these websites, go to the Usborne Quicklinks Website at **www.usborne-quicklinks.com** Read the internet safety guidelines, and then type the keywords "**beginners planet earth**".

The websites are regularly reviewed and the links in Usborne Quicklinks are updated. However, Usborne Publishing is not responsible, and does not accept liability, for the content or availability of any website other than its own. We recommend that children are supervised while on the internet.

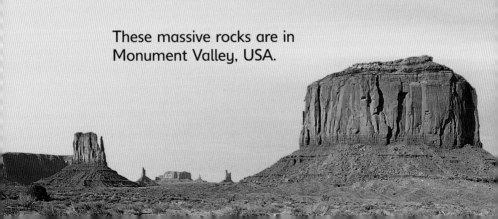

These massive rocks are in Monument Valley, USA.

Index

Africa, 15, 26, 29
Antarctica, 20, 21, 29
caves, 18-19
coast, 22-23
core, 5
crust, 5, 6, 8, 10, 12
deserts, 26-27, 28, 30
earthquakes, 6-7
Europe, 8, 29
faults, 6, 30
icebergs, 20-21, 30
lava, 10, 11, 12, 30
mantle, 5, 10
mountains, 8-9, 14, 29
North America, 17, 28, 31
rivers, 14-15, 16, 17, 18, 30
rocks, 5, 8, 10, 12-13, 14, 18, 19, 22, 23, 26, 30
sand, 13, 22, 23
seas and oceans, 14, 15, 20, 21, 22, 23, 24-25, 29, 30
Sun, 3, 4
volcanoes, 10-11, 12, 23, 30
wearing away, 16-17, 18, 23

Acknowledgements

Additional design by Helen Wood and Erica Harrison
Map illustration page 28-29 by Craig Asquith, European Map Graphics Ltd.
Photographic manipulation by John Russell

Photo credits
The publishers are grateful to the following for permission to reproduce material:
© **BRUCE COLEMAN INC./Alamy** cover; © **Digital Vision** 31; © **Frans Lemmens/zefa/Corbis** 26-27;
© **Gabe Palmer/CORBIS** 1; © **Henry Westheim Photography/Alamy** 7; © **image broker/Alamy** 18-19;
© **Jim Sugar/Corbis** 10; © **Joel Simon/Digital Vision** 20-21; © **Joseph Sohm/Visions of America/Corbis** 13; © **Marc Garanger/CORBIS** 8-9 © **Michael Howard/Alamy** 22-23; © **NASA** 2-3, 5; © **Photo by Rod Catanach, Woods Hole Oceanographic Institution** 25; © **Ron Watts/CORBIS** 17

Every effort has been made to trace and acknowledge ownership of copyright. If any rights have been omitted, the publishers offer to rectify this in any subsequent editions following notification.

First published in 2007 by Usborne Publishing Ltd., Usborne House, 83-85 Saffron Hill, London EC1N 8RT, England. www.usborne.com Copyright © 2007 Usborne Publishing Ltd. The name Usborne and the devices ♀ ☺ are Trade Marks of Usborne Publishing Ltd. All rights reserved. No part of this publication may be reproduced, stored in a retrieval system, or transmitted in any form or by any means, electronic, mechanical, photocopying, recording or otherwise without the prior permission of the publisher. First published in America 2007. U.E. Printed in China.

Your Body

Stephanie Turnbull

Designed by Laura Parker and Michelle Lawrence

Illustrated by Adam Larkum

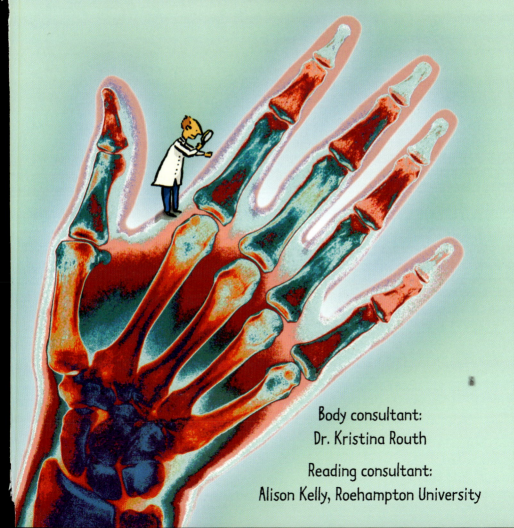

Body consultant:
Dr. Kristina Routh

Reading consultant:
Alison Kelly, Roehampton University

Contents

3 Your amazing body
4 Bony frame
6 Mighty muscles
8 Breathing
10 Powerful pump
12 Inside your head
14 Passing messages
16 Eyes and seeing
18 Ears and hearing
20 Munching machine
22 Where food goes
24 Water works
26 Outer covering
28 Under attack
30 Glossary of body words
31 Websites to visit
32 Index

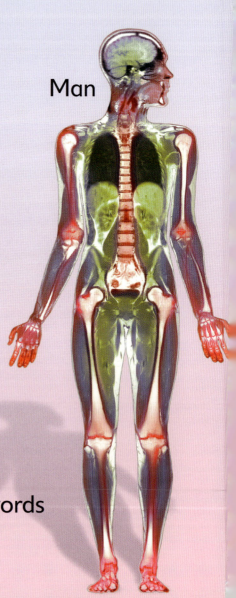

Man

Your amazing body

Your body is like a complicated machine, always working to keep you alive.

Computer scans can show the different parts that make up a person's body.

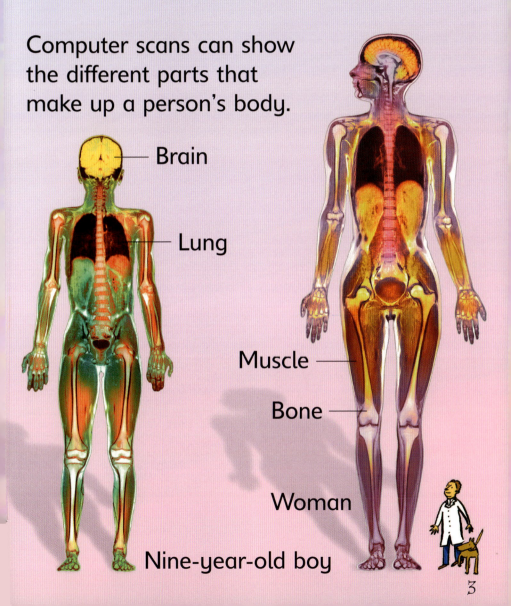

Brain

Lung

Muscle

Bone

Woman

Nine-year-old boy

Bony frame

Your skeleton is a frame of bones that gives your body shape and covers its soft parts.

You were born with about 300 bones. Many of them join together as you grow.

Femur

Adults have 206 bones.
Femurs are the biggest bones.

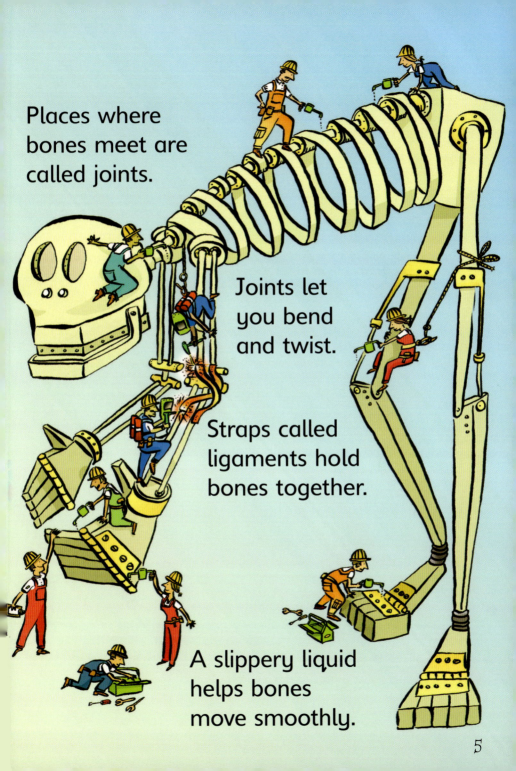

Places where bones meet are called joints.

Joints let you bend and twist.

Straps called ligaments hold bones together.

A slippery liquid helps bones move smoothly.

Mighty muscles

Muscles are rubbery and stretchy. They are often attached across two bones and help the bones move.

When one muscle tightens, it makes a bone move.

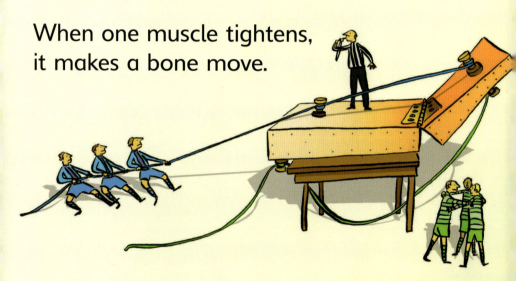

Then another muscle tightens to move the bone back.

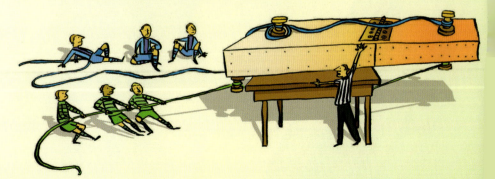

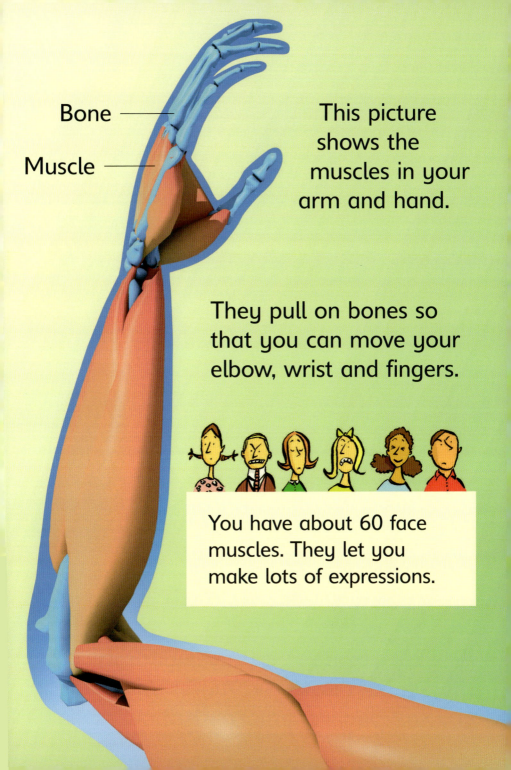

Bone

Muscle

This picture shows the muscles in your arm and hand.

They pull on bones so that you can move your elbow, wrist and fingers.

You have about 60 face muscles. They let you make lots of expressions.

Breathing

Your body needs a gas called oxygen from the air. You get oxygen by breathing air in through your nose and mouth.

Air goes down a tube called the windpipe.

Air fills two big, spongy bags inside you called lungs.

Then a muscle moves up and air is pushed out again.

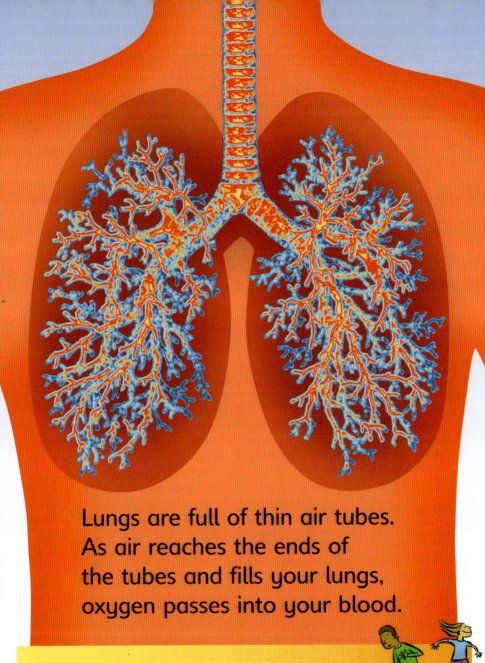

Lungs are full of thin air tubes. As air reaches the ends of the tubes and fills your lungs, oxygen passes into your blood.

When you exercise, your body needs more oxygen, so you breathe faster.

Powerful pump

Your heart is a big, strong muscle that pumps blood around your body.

Blood flows in and out of the heart through tubes.

The tubes go all over your body.

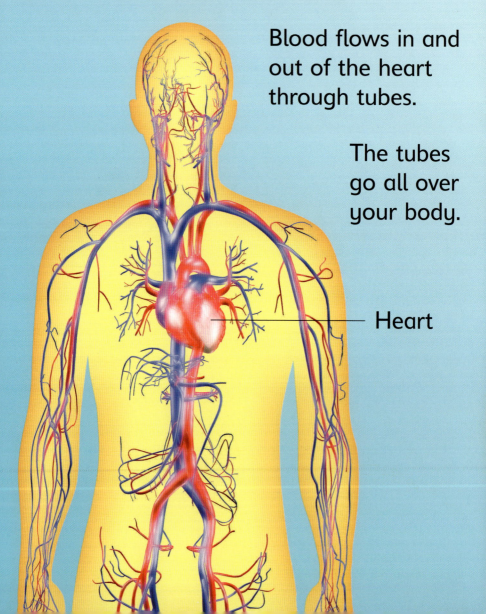

Heart

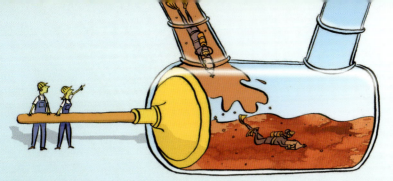

Blood flows into the heart. It is carrying oxygen that it collected from the lungs.

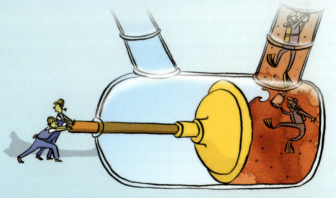

The heart pumps out the blood. This sends the blood rushing around the body.

The blood takes oxygen to every part of the body, then goes back to the heart.

Inside your head

Your brain takes up most of the space in your head. It controls everything in your body, and lets you think and learn.

The wrinkled, orange area in this photograph is a person's brain.

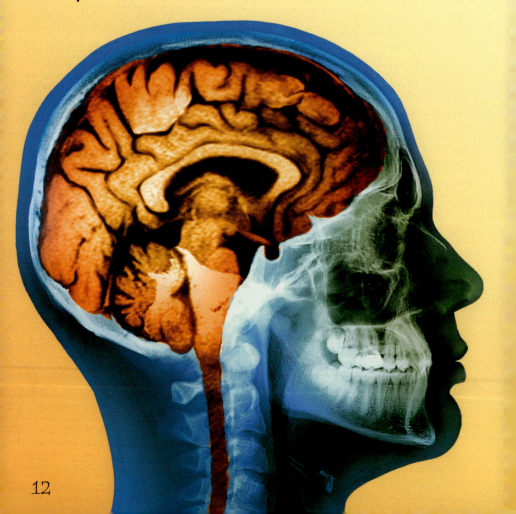

Here are a few of the things that your brain controls.

Smelling

Feeling hungry

Moving

Hearing

Learning and remembering

Seeing

Dreams might be caused by your brain sorting out thoughts while you sleep.

Passing messages

Your brain is connected to every part of your body by tiny threads called nerves.

Nerves pass messages to and from the brain.

This is what a nerve looks like.

It has feathery feelers that touch other nerves to pass messages.

Eyes and seeing

Eyes collect pictures of things around you then nerves send the pictures to the brain.

The brain works out what you are seeing.

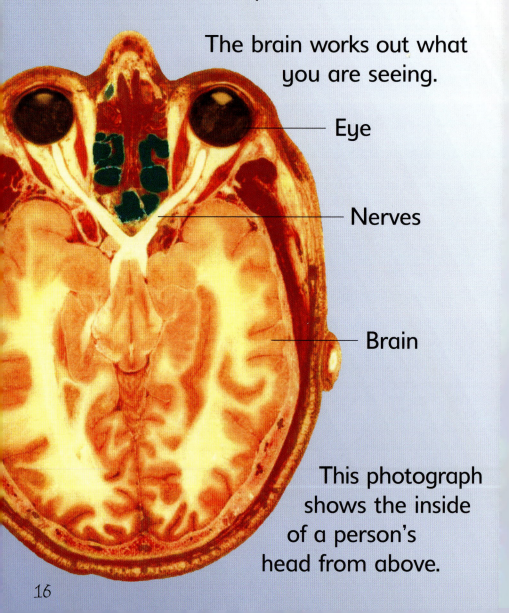

— Eye

— Nerves

— Brain

This photograph shows the inside of a person's head from above.

Light goes in each eye through an opening called the pupil.   Pupil

A thin layer of water keeps eyes clean so that you can see clearly.

When you blink, your eyelids wipe water over each eye.

Any specks of dirt are washed out.

Ears and hearing

Ears go deep inside your head. The part you can see is a flap where sounds go in.

The ear flap collects sounds from the air.

1. Sounds go into your ear and reach a thin piece of skin called the eardrum.

2. Your eardrum starts to wobble, which makes three small bones shake.

Sound is measured in decibels. The sound of a whisper is about 30 decibels. A plane taking off is 140 decibels.

3. The shaking makes a liquid move deep in the ear. Hairs in the liquid sway.

4. Nerves in the hairs send messages about the sounds to the brain.

Munching machine

When you eat, your lips, teeth and tongue work together to break up food.

Teeth are covered in a hard coating called enamel.

They have roots that go deep into your gums.

——— Root
——— Tooth

Enamel is the hardest material in your body.

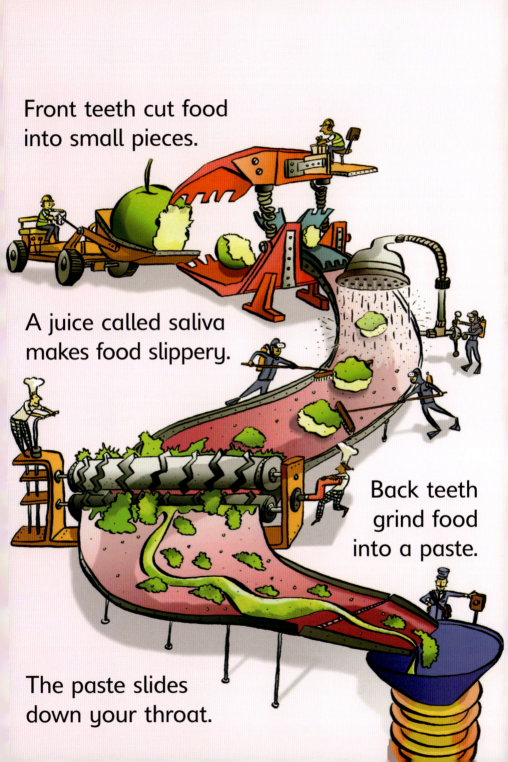

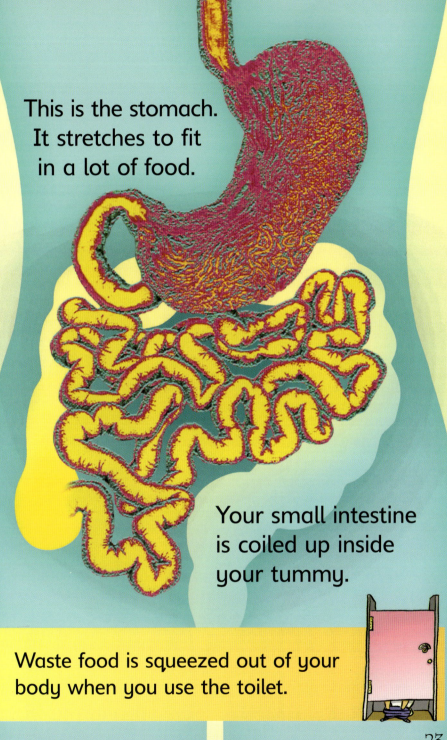

This is the stomach. It stretches to fit in a lot of food.

Your small intestine is coiled up inside your tummy.

Waste food is squeezed out of your body when you use the toilet.

Water works

Your body needs to get rid of extra water that builds up in the blood. This job is done by your two kidneys.

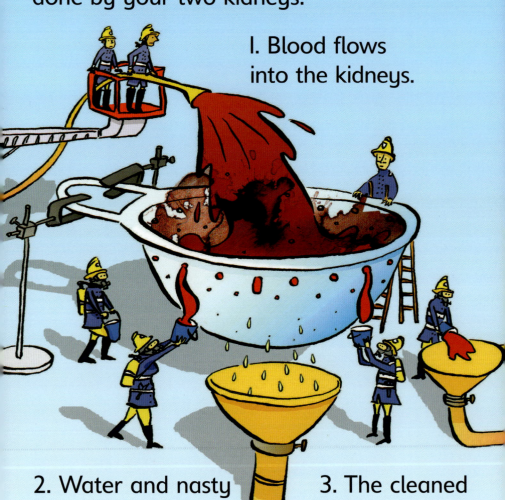

1. Blood flows into the kidneys.

2. Water and nasty chemicals drain out of each kidney.

3. The cleaned blood continues around the body.

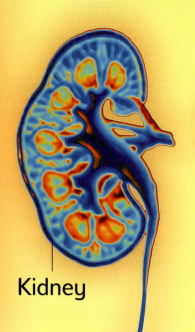

Kidney

Waste water trickles down tubes and into a bag called the bladder.

When the bladder is full, you go to the toilet to empty it.

Bladder

In just four minutes, all the blood in your body passes through your kidneys to be cleaned.

Outer covering

Skin holds your body together and gives you a waterproof covering. It is made up of layers.

Top layers of skin get worn away. New layers grow underneath.

Hairs grow up from roots deep in the bottom layer.

The bottom layer is fatty and soft.

Under attack

Tiny harmful things called germs are always trying to invade your body.

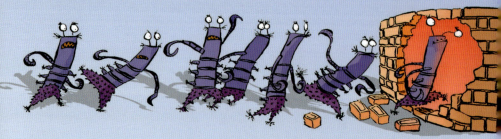

Germs often get inside your body through cuts and scratches.

White blood cells in your blood find the germs and zap them with chemicals.

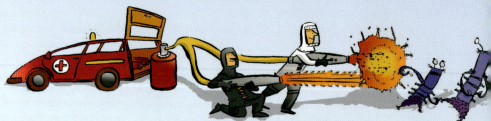

A doctor might give you medicine or pills that contain extra chemicals to fight germs.

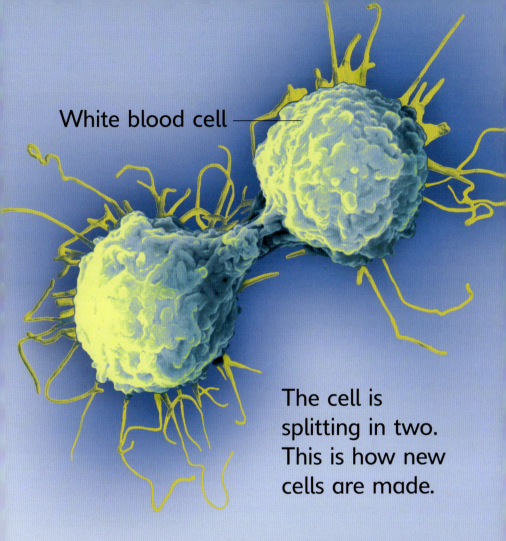

White blood cell

The cell is splitting in two. This is how new cells are made.

This is what white blood cells look like under a powerful microscope. Their long strands help them cling onto things.

If germs in your body are too strong to be killed, they can make you sick.

Glossary of body words

Here are some of the words in this book you might not know. This page tells you what they mean.

 ligament - A tough, stretchy band that holds two bones together.

 oxygen - An invisible gas in the air. Your body needs oxygen to work.

 saliva - Liquid in your mouth that makes food soft and easy to swallow.

 stomach - A strong, stretchy bag where food is turned into a mushy mixture.

 nerve - A thin thread that passes messages to and from your brain.

 germ - A tiny living thing that can get into your body and make you sick.

 white blood cell - A very small speck in your blood that fights germs.

Websites to visit

You can visit exciting websites to find out more about your body.

To visit these websites, go to the Usborne Quicklinks Website at **www.usborne-quicklinks.com** Read the internet safety guidelines, and then type the keywords "**beginners body**".

The websites are regularly reviewed and the links in Usborne Quicklinks are updated. However, Usborne Publishing is not responsible, and does not accept liability, for the content or availability of any website other than its own. We recommend that children are supervised while on the internet.

This is what a group of germs looks like under a microscope.

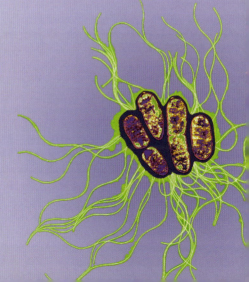

Index

bladder, 25
blood, 9, 10, 11, 24
bones, 3, 4, 5, 6, 7, 18,
brain, 3, 12, 13, 14, 15,
   16, 19
breathing, 8, 9
eardrum, 18
ears, 18, 19
eating, 13, 20, 21, 22, 23
eyes, 16, 17
germs, 28, 29, 30
hairs, 19, 26, 27
hearing, 13, 18, 19
heart, 10, 11
joints, 5, 6
kidneys, 24, 25
ligaments, 5, 30

lungs, 3, 8, 9, 11
moving, 5, 6, 7, 13
muscles, 3, 6, 7, 8, 10
nerves, 14, 15, 16, 19, 30
oxygen, 8, 9, 11, 30
saliva, 21, 30
seeing, 13, 16, 17
skeleton, 4, 5
skin, 26, 27
small intestine, 22, 23
smelling, 13
stomach, 22, 23, 30
sweat, 27
teeth, 20, 21
white blood cells, 28,
   29, 30
windpipe, 8

Acknowledgements

Photographic manipulation by John Russell

Photo credits

The publishers are grateful to the following for permission to reproduce material:
© **Alamy** 7 (ImageDJ); © **Corbis** 1 (Firefly Productions); © **Getty Images** 17 (Bob Elsdale);
© **Science Photo Library** 2-3 (Simon Fraser), 4, 9, 10, 23, 25, (Alfred Pasieka),
12 (Sovereign, ISM), 14 (Dr. Torsten Wittmann), 16 (Mehau Kulyk), 20 (D. Roberts),
29 (Stem Jems), 31 (Dr. Linda Stannard, UCT).

Every effort has been made to trace and acknowledge ownership of copyright. If any rights have been omitted, the publishers offer to rectify this in any subsequent editions following notification.

First published in 2005 by Usborne Publishing Ltd., Usborne House, 83-85 Saffron Hill, London EC1N 8RT, England. www.usborne.com Copyright © 2007, 2005 Usborne Publishing Ltd. The name Usborne and the devices ♀ ⊕ are Trade Marks of Usborne Publishing Ltd. All rights reserved. No part of this publication may be reproduced, stored in a retrieval system, or transmitted in any form or by any means, electronic, mechanical, photocopying, recording or otherwise without the prior permission of the publisher. First published in America 2005. U.E. Printed in China.

Astronomy

Emily Bone

Designed by Matthew Preston and Sam Chandler
Illustrated by John Fox and Uta Bettzieche

Astronomy consultant: Dr. Leila Powell
Reading consultant: Alison Kelly

Contents

- 3 Studying the sky
- 4 What's in space?
- 6 A place in space
- 8 Watching space
- 10 Telescopes in space
- 12 Looking at galaxies
- 14 The Milky Way
- 16 Studying stars
- 18 The Sun
- 20 Probing planets
- 22 Exploring the surface
- 24 The Moon
- 26 Space lumps
- 28 Stargazing
- 30 Glossary
- 31 Internet links
- 32 Index

Studying the sky

When you look up at the night sky, you might see lots of stars. This is only a tiny part of space.

Astronomers study space to find out about the different things that are found there.

What's in space?

There are lots of different things in space.

Planets are big, round lumps of rock or balls of gases.

Some have rocky or icy moons moving around them.

Smaller pieces of rock or ice are called asteroids.

Stars are massive balls of gases. Many have planets moving around them.

Millions and millions of stars are grouped together in galaxies...

...and there are millions and millions of galaxies in space.

A place in space

Planet Earth is one of eight planets that move around a star called the Sun.

The Sun and planets are known as the Solar System.

The planets in the Solar System are very far apart. They're very different sizes, too.

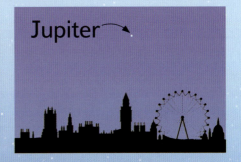

Jupiter is the biggest planet. This is how big Jupiter is compared to Earth.

Jupiter is so far away from Earth, it looks like a bright star in the sky.

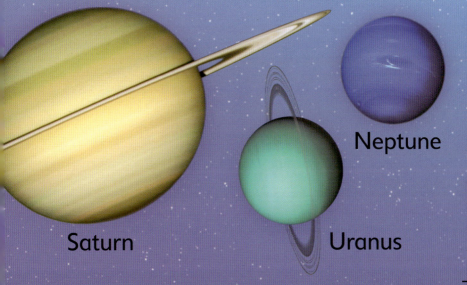

Saturn

Uranus

Neptune

Watching space

Astronomers use telescopes to get clear pictures of things that are in space. There are lots of different types of telescopes.

Radio telescopes find planets, stars and galaxies by collecting signals from space.

These are some of the ALMA radio telescopes in Chile, South America.

The Keck telescopes in Hawaii, U.S.A., use huge, curved mirrors and cameras to make pictures.

At night, light from a planet is reflected from the mirrors into the cameras.

The cameras turn this light into a clear picture of the planet.

Telescopes in space

Some telescopes fly around the Earth in space. The Hubble telescope is a famous space telescope.

Big mirrors on Hubble reflect light coming from distant galaxies.

A camera takes pictures of the galaxies and measures how far away they are.

Hubble sends signals to radio dishes on Earth. The dishes send signals to computers.

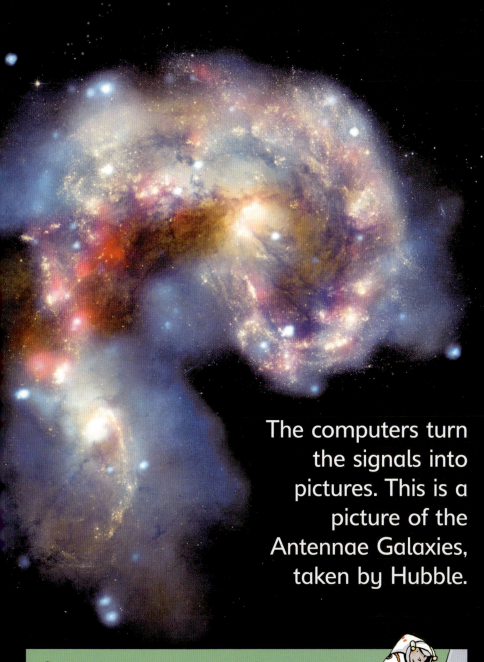

The computers turn the signals into pictures. This is a picture of the Antennae Galaxies, taken by Hubble.

Sometimes, astronauts have to go into space to fix Hubble.

Looking at galaxies

Astronomers have discovered different types of galaxies.

Some galaxies are shaped like a spiral. This picture of a spiral galaxy was taken by the Hubble telescope.

Other galaxies are known as irregular galaxies. These can be different shapes.

The Cartwheel Galaxy looks like a wheel.

Some galaxies are slowly joining together.

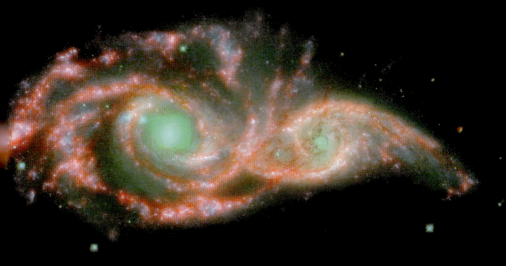

These two spiral galaxies will eventually become one even bigger galaxy.

The Milky Way

The Solar System is part of a galaxy known as the Milky Way.

Astronomers pointed the Spitzer space telescope at stars in the Milky Way.

This is Spitzer. It's around the same size as Hubble.

A camera on Spitzer took pictures of different stars.

It sent this information to computers on Earth.

The computers used signals from Spitzer to make a big picture of the Milky Way.

The Solar System is around here.

Astonomers are looking for planets in the Milky Way outside our Solar System.

Studying stars

Stars form inside a swirling cloud of gas and dust, called a nebula.

Astronomers use telescopes to study how stars form.

This is a picture of the Carina Nebula taken by the Hubble space telescope.

The bright points of light inside the nebula are new stars.

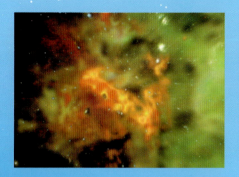 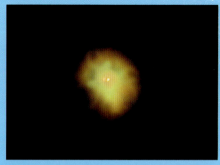

Gas and dust in part of the nebula start to form a clump. It gets hotter.

Gradually, the hot clump becomes a bright, glowing ball. This is a star.

The star glows for millions of years. Slowly, it gets bigger and redder.

Eventually, layers of gas puff off into space, and the star fades away.

The biggest stars end in a huge explosion called a supernova.

The Sun

The Sun is the closest star to Earth. Astronomers study the Sun using the SOHO space telescope. It flies around the Sun in space.

SOHO took this picture of the Sun.

Never ever look directly at the Sun. Its strong light could hurt your eyes.

This is a close-up picture taken from SOHO of a huge loop of gas on the Sun.

SOHO blocks out the Sun's light to detect hot gas around the Sun, called a corona.

It also photographs sunspots, which are cooler patches on the Sun's surface.

Probing planets

A probe is a type of spacecraft that flies to planets. It takes lots of pictures and sends them back to computers on Earth.

This is a probe called Voyager 2. It took this picture of Neptune.

The probe found dark swirls on the planet. These are huge storms.

Venus is covered in thick clouds. The Magellan probe used signals to make pictures of the surface.

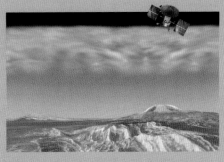

The Magellan probe sent signals through the clouds.

The signals bounced off the surface, then back up to the probe.

A computer used the signals to make this picture of the surface.

Exploring the surface

Rovers are vehicles that explore planets. They drive around, taking pictures of the surface and studying rocks.

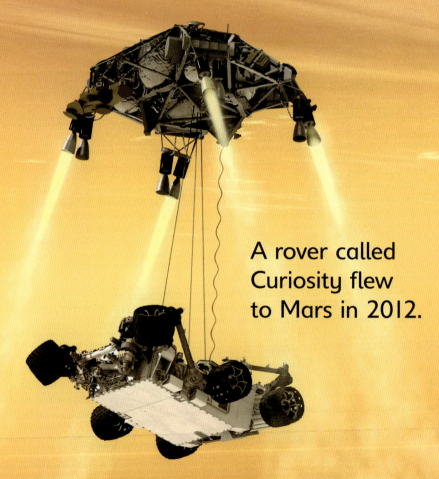

A rover called Curiosity flew to Mars in 2012.

This is how Curiosity looked as it was lowered to the surface by a spacecraft.

Curiosity has studied different rocks to look for signs of water.

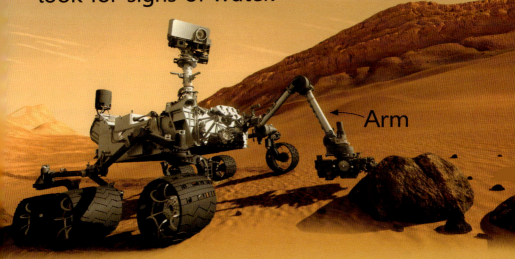

Arm

A drill on the end of Curiosity's arm made a hole in a rock. This made lots of dust.

It moved its arm to scoop up dust, then tested it.

It sent the results of the tests back to astronomers on Earth.

The Moon

The Earth has a smaller, rocky ball moving around it, called the Moon.

As the Moon moves, the Sun lights up different parts of it, so it looks as though it's changing shape each night.

When you can only see a small part of the Moon, it's called a Crescent Moon.

For over 50 years, astronomers have used spacecraft to find out about the Moon.

In 1959, a Russian spacecraft flew around the Moon and took pictures.

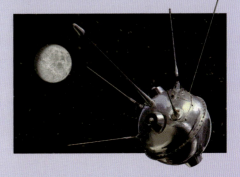

Astronauts landed on the Moon in 1969. They took rocks back to Earth.

Astronomers sent a probe to the Moon to study its soil in 2009.

In the future, people might live on the Moon.

Space lumps

Asteroids are lumps of rock, ice or metal in space. Sometimes, they crash into Earth.

Some rocks heat up as they move close to the Earth.

They get hotter and hotter until they catch fire.

All the rock and metal burns up, leaving just a streak of light in the sky.

Other rocks don't burn up. They hit the Earth instead. Astronomers study them to find out about rocks in space.

This rock landed on Earth. It's shown here at around twice its actual size.

It's been cut open to see what's inside. The shiny pieces inside the rock are metal.

When some space rocks hit Earth, they make holes called craters.

Stargazing

You can see lots of different things in the night sky without using a telescope.

Some stars look like patterns in the sky. They are called constellations.

This constellation is Canis Major. If the stars are joined by lines, it looks like a dog.

Constellations can look different when you see them from different places on the Earth.

Sometimes, glowing lights appear in the sky. This is called an aurora.

A comet is a lump of dust and ice. It has a bright tail that can be seen from Earth.

The bright strip of stars in this picture is the middle of the Milky Way galaxy.

Glossary

Here are some of the words in this book you might not know. This page tells you what they mean.

 star - a huge ball of gases in space. The Sun is a star.

 galaxy - a group of millions and millions of stars.

 telescope - equipment that makes things that are far away seem larger.

 nebula - a swirling cloud of gas and dust where stars form.

 probe - a spacecraft for exploring planets that is controlled by a computer.

 rover - a computer-controlled vehicle that drives across a planet.

 constellation - stars in the night sky that look like a pattern.

Websites to visit

You can visit exciting websites to find out more about astronomy.

To visit these websites, go to the Usborne Quicklinks Website at **www.usborne-quicklinks.com**

Read the internet safety guidelines, and then type the keywords "**beginners astronomy**".

The websites are regularly reviewed and the links in Usborne Quicklinks are updated. However, Usborne Publishing is not responsible, and does not accept liability, for the content or availability of any website other than its own. We recommend that children are supervised while on the internet.

This is a picture of the Tycho Supernova taken by the Spitzer space telescope.

Index

aurora, 29
asteroids, 4, 26-27
astronauts, 11, 25
comets, 29
constellations, 28, 30
Earth, 6, 10, 23, 26, 27, 28, 29
galaxies, 5, 8, 10, 11, 12-13, 14, 15, 30
Milky Way, 14-15, 28-29
moons, 4, 24-25
nebula, 16, 17, 30
night sky, 3, 7, 9, 26, 28-29
planets, 4, 6, 7, 8, 9, 15, 20, 21, 22, 23
probes, 20-21, 25, 30
rovers, 22-23, 30
Solar System, 6-7, 14, 15
stars, 3, 4, 5, 6, 7, 8, 14, 16-17, 28, 29, 30
Sun, 6, 18-19, 24
supernova, 17, 31
telescopes, 8-9, 10-11, 12, 14, 16, 18, 19, 30

Acknowledgements

Photographic manipulation by John Russell

Photo credits

The publishers are grateful to the following for permission to reproduce material: cover © STScI/NASA (Hubble space telescope); © J. Hester, P. Scowen (ASU), HST, NASA (Eagle Nebula); p1 © NASA (New Horizons space probe); p2-3 © David Nunuk/Getty Images; p4 © NASA, ESA, and the Hubble Heritage Team (STScI/AURA); p5 © the Hubble Heritage Team (AURA/ STScI/ NASA) (galaxy); © R. Williams (STScI), the Hubble Deep Field Team and NASA (galaxy group); p6-7 © Hubble Heritage Team, D. Gouliermis (MPI Heidelberg) et al., (STScI/AURA), ESA, NASA (starry background); p6 © SOHO (ESA & NASA) (The Sun) © Lunar and Planetary Institute (Mercury); © NASA/JPL (Venus and Mars); © NASA (Earth); © NASA/JPL/University of Arizona (Jupiter); p7 © NASA/JPL/STSI (Saturn); © William Radcliffe/Science Faction/Corbis (Uranus); © NASA (Neptune); p8 © Babak Tafreshi, TWAN/ Science Photo Library; p9 © Richard Wainscoat/Alamy (Keck telescopes); © NASA/JPL/University of Arizona (Jupiter); p10 and 11 © NASA, ESA, and the Hubble Heritage Team (STScI/AURA)-ESA/Hubble Collaboration; p12 © X-ray: NASA/CXC/Wisconsin/D.Pooley and CfA/A.Zezas; Optical: NASA/ESA/ CfA/A.Zezas; UV: NASA/JPL-Caltech/CfA/J.Huchra et al.; IR: NASA/JPL-Caltech/CfA; p13 © NASA/ JPL-Caltech (irregular galaxy); © NASA/JPL-Caltech/STScI/Vassar (merging galaxy); p15 © NASA/JPL-Caltech; p16-17 © NASA, ESA, and the Hubble SM4 ERO Team; p17 © NASA, ESA, HEIC, and The Hubble Heritage Team (STScI/AURA); p18, 19 © NASA/SDO (whole Sun and solar flare); p19 © ESA/ NASA/epa/Corbis (corona); © SOHO/ESA/NASA/Science Photo Library (sunspots); p20 © NASA/JPL (Neptune); © NASA/JPL-Caltech (Voyager 2 probe); p21 © NASA/JPL (Venus surface probe step); © NASA/ JPL; p22 © NASA; p23 © NASA/JPL-Caltech/Science Photo Library; p24 © NASA/GSFC-SVS/Science Photo Library; p25 © NASA Images/Alamy (astronaut on Moon); p26 © Thomas Heaton/Science Photo Library; p27 © NASA/Science Photo Library; p28-29 © Mike Hollingshead/Science Faction/ SuperStock; p30 © NASA/SDO (Sun); © NASA, ESA, and the Hubble Heritage Team (STScI/AURA)-ESA/Hubble Collaboration (galaxy); © NASA, ESA, HEIC, and The Hubble Heritage Team (STScI/ AURA) (nebula); p31 © X-ray: NASA/CXC/SAO; Infrared: NASA/JPL-Caltech; Optical: MPIA, Calar Alto, O. Krause et al.

Every effort has been made to trace and acknowledge ownership of copyright. If any rights have been omitted, the publishers offer to rectify this in any subsequent editions following notification.

First published in 2014 by Usborne Publishing Ltd., Usborne House, 83-85 Saffron Hill, London EC1N 8RT, England. www.usborne.com Copyright © 2014 Usborne Publishing Ltd. The name Usborne and the devices ♛ are Trade Marks of Usborne Publishing Ltd. All rights reserved. No part of this publication may be reproduced, stored in a retrieval system, or transmitted in any form or by any means, electronic, mechanical, photocopying, recording or otherwise without the prior permission of the publisher. First published in America 2014. U.E.